PERSONALITY DEVELOPMENT

Core concepts in therapy

Series editor: Michael Jacobs

Over the last ten years a significant shift has taken place in the relations between representatives of different schools of therapy. Instead of the competitive and often hostile reactions we once expected from each other, therapists from different points along the spectrum of approaches are much more interested in where they overlap and where they differ. There is a new sense of openness to cross-orientation learning.

The *Core Concepts in Therapy* series compares and contrasts the use of similar terms across a range of the therapeutic models, and seeks to identify where different terms appear to denote similar concepts. Each book is authored by two therapists, each one from a distinctly different orientation; and where possible each one from a different continent, so that an international dimension becomes a feature of this network of ideas.

Each of these short volumes examines a key concept in psychological therapy, setting out comparative positions in a spirit of free and critical enquiry, but without the need to prove one model superior to another. The books are fully referenced and point beyond themselves to the wider literature on each topic.

List of forthcoming and published titles:

PERSONALITY DEVELOPMENT

Valerie Simanowitz
and
Peter Pearce

Open University Press

Open University Press
McGraw-Hill Education
McGraw-Hill House
Shoppenhangers Road
Maidenhead
Berkshire
England
SL6 2QL

email: enquiries@openup.co.uk
world wide web: www.openup.co.uk

First published 2003

A catalogue record of this book is available from the British Library

ISBN 0 335 20635 2 (pb)   0 335 20636 0 (hb)

Library of Congress Cataloging-in-Publication Data
CIP data has been applied for

Typeset by RefineCatch Limited, Bungay, Suffolk
Printed in Great Britain by MPG Books Ltd, Bodmin, Cornwall

Contents

Acknowledgements

For help, support, generosity and encouragement from Arnold Simanowitz, Philippa Donald, Sue Daniels, John Barry (Brighton University Library) and Leni Gillman.

Series editor's preface

A major aspect of intellectual and cultural life in the twentieth century has been the study of psychology – present of course for many centuries in practical form and expression in the wisdom and insight to be found in spirituality, in literature and in the dramatic arts, as well as in arts of healing and guidance, both in the East and West. In parallel with the deepening interest in the inner processes of character and relationships in the novel and theatre in the nineteenth century, psychiatry reformulated its understanding of the human mind, and encouraged, in those brave enough to challenge the myths of mental illness, new methods of exploration of psychological processes.

The second half of the twentieth century in particular witnessed an explosion of interest both in theories about personality, psychological development, cognition and behaviour, as well as in the practice of therapy, or perhaps more accurately, the therapies. It also saw, as is not uncommon in any intellectual discipline, battles between theories and therapists of different persuasions, particularly between psychoanalysis and behavioural psychology, and each in turn with humanistic and transpersonal therapies, as well as within the major schools themselves. Such arguments are not surprising, and indeed objectively can be seen as healthy – potentially promoting greater precision in research, alternative approaches to apparently intractable problems, and deeper understanding of the wellsprings of human thought, emotion and behaviour. It is nonetheless disturbing that for many decades there was such a degree of sniping and entrenchment of positions from therapists who should have been able to look more closely at their own responses and rivalries. It is as if diplomats had ignored their skills and knowledge and resorted in their dealings with each other to gun slinging.

The psychotherapeutic enterprise has also been an international one. There were a large number of centres of innovation, even at the beginning – Paris, Moscow, Vienna, Berlin, Zurich, London, Boston USA – and soon Edinburgh, Rome, New York, Chicago and California saw the development of different theories and therapeutic practice. Geographical location has added to the richness of the discipline, particularly identifying cultural and social differences, and widening the psychological debate to include, at least in some instances, sociological and political dimensions.

The question has to be asked – given the separate developments due to location, research interests, personal differences, and splits between and within traditions – whether what has sometimes been called 'psycho-babble' is indeed a welter of different languages describing the same phenomena through the particular jargon and theorizing of the various psychotherapeutic schools. Or are there genuine differences, which may lead sometimes to the conclusion that one school has got it right, while another has therefore got it wrong; or that there are 'horses for courses'; or, according to the Dodo principle, that 'all shall have prizes'?

The latter part of the twentieth century saw some rapprochement between the different approaches to the theory and practice of psychotherapy (and counselling), often due to the external pressures towards organizing the profession responsibly and to the high standards demanded of it by health care, by the public, and by the state. It is out of this budding rapprochement that there came the motivation for this series, in which a number of key concepts that lie at the heart of the psychotherapies can be compared and contrasted across the board. Some of the terms used in different traditions may prove to represent identical concepts; others may look similar, but in fact highlight quite different emphases, which may or may not prove useful to those who practise from a different perspective; other terms, apparently identical, may prove to mean something completely different in two or more schools of psychotherapy.

In order to carry out this project it seemed essential that as many of the psychotherapeutic traditions as possible should be represented in the authorship of the series; and to promote both this, and the spirit of dialogue between traditions, it seemed also desirable that there should be two authors for each book, each one representing, where practicable, different orientations. It was important that the series should be truly international in its approach and therefore in its authorship; and that miracle of late twentieth-century technology, the Internet, proved to be a productive means of finding authors, as well as a remarkably efficient method of communicating, in the cases of some pairs of authors, halfway across the world.

This series therefore represents, in a new millennium, an extremely exciting development, one which as series editor I have found more and more enthralling as I have eavesdropped on the drafts shuttling back and forth between authors. Here, for the first time, the reader will find all the major concepts of all the principal schools of psychotherapy and counselling (and not a few minor ones) drawn together so that they may be compared, contrasted, and (it is my hope) above all used – used for the ongoing debate between orientations, but more importantly still, used for the benefit of clients and patients who are not at all interested in partisan positions, but in what works, or in what throws light upon their search for healing and understanding.

Michael Jacobs

Preface

What is character but the determination of incident? what is incident but the determination of character?

Henry James

Since ancient times people have been fascinated to discover how they came to possess their personal characteristics and qualities, and have wanted to know what causes such infinite variety within and between people, even those raised in the same family, class and culture. As counsellors and therapists it is intrinsic to our work that we have a curiosity about how we and our clients came to be the people we are: thus much of our work, consciously or unconsciously, is informed by models of personality development.

This book is about some of the different models that have been created to describe the development of personality. It considers how each model conceptualizes what constitutes normal human development and what processes lead to an individual acquiring the relatively stable set of traits and attributes given the term 'personality'. Personality has been a somewhat controversial concept psychologically, going in and out of favour despite continuing to have a ready meaning in popular culture. Other books in this series examine ways of describing personality types (Totton and Jacobs 2001), or the structure of personality (Brinich and Shelley 2002). In this book we examine explanations of how people may have come to be the way they are.

Any professional training in counselling and psychotherapy needs to devote time to an exploration of ideas about what constitutes normal human development, and what can impact on this process. Whether our chosen therapeutic approach is interested in the past, or is present and future focused, we still need to examine our beliefs about how people might begin to struggle with life and how they came to be involved with some of the issues they bring to therapy.

Beliefs about development and personality also shape our ideas about how to respond to these issues, and therefore define what the role and focus of the therapist might be.

A grounding in theories of development can also serve as a solid foundation from which to compare our own belief system and practice with that of practitioners from other approaches. In the context of increasing integration it can thus serve to ensure coherence between theory and practice, and prevent the sort of faddish eclecticism that was rightly criticized by Hans Eysenck as far back as the 1960s.

Furthermore, if as counsellors and therapists we have not examined our own (perhaps implicit) assumptions about what constitutes 'normal' development, we may unwittingly impose these unexamined beliefs on our clients or offer contradictory ideas about how therapy could be of benefit to them.

As therapists both authors are happiest to be positioned within the person-centred school, although Peter's training has been broader, including psychodynamic, systemic and integrative perspectives. This has been partially as a result of his working within an NHS multi-disciplinary community team setting since 1988. In this setting it has been important to be able to learn a variety of 'therapeutic languages' to enable dialogue between different professions and approaches. The premise of this series attracted our involvement: that counselling and psychotherapy are now themselves sufficiently 'grown up' and socially accepted to be able to put to one side the history of sectarianism, and become interested in how different approaches make sense of the human condition. We both believe strongly that providing potential clients with clear knowledge about the ideas underpinning approaches is desirable and necessary if we are truly committed as a profession to empowering our clients and demystifying the practice of therapy. Here we need to draw the distinction between the illusory 'choice' that is offered by the myriad models of therapy and 'effective choice', which requires sufficient information to enable understanding as well as the power to gain access to a person's chosen therapy.

The outline of the text is as follows. Chapter one examines psychoanalytic models of personality development. It begins with Freud's key theories, which initially emphasized psychosexual development and the gratification of needs. It then traces the key historical developments and contemporary psychodynamic theories of personality development, including the theories put forward by Melanie Klein, W.R.D. Fairbairn, D.W. Winnicott, Margart Mahler, John Bowlby, Heinz Kohut and Daniel Stern.

Chapter two examines the life stage models of both Erik H. Erikson and Daniel Levinson. A detailed overview is given of Erikson's theory of ego development through eight life stages with his emphasis on adolescence and identity. Although Erikson could have been viewed as belonging within the psychodynamic chapter, we have addressed his work separately, as his emphasis is less intra-psychic and more interpersonal. He pays attention to the importance of social development. Levinson divides the seasons of a person's life into eras and transitions. A detailed overview is given of these five developmental eras, and they are contrasted with Erikson's model. Levinson's focus is more on the middle stages of life. His ideas, like Erikson's, consider both the person and the nature of society providing a complex view of adulthood. His model is hierarchical with a progression that requires that the task for each stage be completed. Erikson's model is also progressive, with each stage building on the one before. Both approaches are perhaps open to the criticism of appearing to suggest that once a stage has been negotiated satisfactorily the basic strength is permanently acquired. However, this suggestion would be misleading. Erikson, for example, specifically suggested that the strength acquired in each stage continues to develop throughout life.

Chapter three considers the person-centred approach developed by Carl Rogers. This is an actualization model in that it views development as ongoing throughout the life cycle. Although academic theorists on personality in the past have not ascribed a comprehensive theory of personality to the person-centred approach, they have failed to recognize that Rogers' 1957 paper in Koch (1989) on the development of personality is very extensive. This chapter also explores developments in person-centred theory such as David Mearns' and Brian Thorne's ideas about different configurations of the self and Mick Cooper's expansions of the theory of development. These attempt to redress the balance between social mediation (the expectations of society) and the actualizing tendency.

Chapter four details the key themes and ideas behind existential theory as they relate to personality development. It is hard to define the core developmental statement of existentialism. Instead we explore the contribution of existential philosophy to our understanding of personality, including some of the ideas of the philosophers Kierkegaard, Nietzsche, Heidegger and Sartre and the psychotherapists Binswanger, Frankl, Boss, May and Yalom. The existential ideas around phenomenology and intersubjectivity have exerted an impact across the different schools of psychotherapy – psychodynamic, humanistic and beyond.

Chapter five examines Lawrence Kohlberg's six-stage theory about the development of moral decision-making. He views this as a developmental task that requires time and the development of the person both mentally and physically. We have included Carol Gilligan's feminist critique of Kohlberg, particularly of his conclusion that women are morally inferior. Gilligan highlights that women's distinctive voice has not been included in studies of human moral development. She further describes the lack of a psychological language to describe women's specific experience. Her ideas about female identity formation in childhood and adolescence are outlined. Women are seen as focusing more on connection and relationships rather than success.

We have tried to write with an awareness of our own world-view, philosophy and sociopolitical context as authors: Val as a white, middle-class, mature woman and Peter as a white, middle-class man. Many previous texts on the development of personality consider only the main theoretical models. In this book we have sought to be more contemporary and representative by including feminist perspectives as well as the development of race identity and spirituality in the course of chapters seven, eight and nine. Again, in aiming to give due voice to a feminist perspective, we have included Gilligan in both chapter six and chapter nine. This last examines Carl Jung, who, unlike Freud and his disciples, considered the spiritual dimension and people's search for meaning as highly significant aspects of the developing personality. It outlines the ideas of Roberto Assagioli, the founder of the psychosynthesis movement, and it seeks to give a concise overview of the ideas of Ken Wilbur, strongly influenced by Eastern philosophy, who has sought to provide specific maps of ascending levels of consciousness.

We are grateful for the contribution of Jarlath Benson, who wrote chapter nine. He is a psychosynthesis trainer and therapist, who has brought his specialist knowledge in the transpersonal field to our book. We are also grateful to Philippa Donald, who was originally going to be the co-author of this book with Val. Philippa is also a psychosynthesis therapist, and her enthusiastic contribution of ideas in the early stages of planning has been important to the development of this book.

Chapter six begins by exploring feminist critiques of the patriarchal attitudes inherent within early psychodynamic and developmental stage theories. The chapter goes on to raise awareness of the patriarchal attitudes that permeate developmental theories more generally. It describes how even influential women theorists like Klein, Horney and Chodorow have tended to accept some of the underlying patriarchal assumptions.

Chapter seven introduces models of racial/ethnic identity development and considers the role played by culture in personality development, for example through internalized racism. The chapter considers how as counsellors and therapists working transculturally we must have an awareness of both our own and our clients' culture.

In our concluding chapter we compare some of the different concepts used to describe personality development and acknowledge the limitations of the different models.

It is our hope that we have provided an accessible text that gives a clear overview of a variety of approaches and can serve as a stimulus to further study for those interested. Although we have provided critiques of most of the theories, we have intentionally not attempted a detailed analysis of the relative merits of each model. To do so would inevitably have meant involving our own interpretations and could therefore have proven more confusing than illuminating for readers.

We have both worked as therapists, supervisors and trainers in an inner-city context and are particularly aware of how traditional theories of personality development fail to meet the needs of a multi-ethnic and diverse community in the twenty-first century. We are aware that the theories have a foundation that is embedded in the culture and consciousness of both trainee and practising therapist; and that while many contain concepts of timeless relevance, some that were radical and innovative when they were written have become outdated and no longer relevant for our age and society. In this book we have tried to maintain the tension between identifying and preserving some core universal concepts while questioning and critiquing them, as well as introducing some alternative models. Perhaps the most that can be said by way of generalization is that none of the models we have examined are carved in stone. The models themselves develop as patterns in society and culture shift. It would be interesting no doubt to trace how far the models reflect cultural norms, and so follow as much as inform our assumptions of how we have come to be the way we are. But that, no doubt, is another book, for another time!

C H A P T E R **1**

Psychoanalytic/psychodynamic developmental theories

Peter Pearce

There has now been more than a hundred years of psychoanalytic theorizing on the development of personality, and there are consequently a variety of different psychodynamic models. Despite sharing common origins, each of these theories has a different emphasis. Some theorists have sought to adapt existing ideas to remain within the psychoanalytic approach, while others have redefined them as distinct and separate.

Sigmund Freud's developmental stage theory

The approach began with the work of Sigmund Freud in Vienna at the end of the nineteenth century. Freud was trained as a medical doctor and applied terms from scientific study to his ideas, endeavouring, particularly early in his career, to give them a biological basis. He coined the term 'psycho-dynamic' to describe the constant tension and conflict between opposing forces within the 'psyche' or internal world.

He outlined a 'structural', tripartite model of the internal (intra-psychic) world, defining three distinct elements: id, ego and superego, or 'it', 'me' and 'above me' (see also in this series Brinich and Shelley, *The Self and Personality Structure*, 2002).

Freud described 'instincts' or 'drives' that were seen as innate, universal and constantly felt.

An instinct differs from a stimulus in that it arises from sources of stimulation within the body, operates as a constant force and is such that the subject cannot escape from it by flight as he can from an external stimulus. An instinct may be described as having a source, an object and an aim. The source is a state of excitation within the body and its aim is to remove that excitation.

(Freud 1938: 125)

For Freud, life was principally concerned with the management of these conflicts, with individuals attempting to maximize instinctual gratification while minimizing guilt and punishment. Freud's approach has, therefore, been described as a conflict management model of the inner world.

Freud initially conceptualized drives (in German, Triebe) as related to the preservation of life (hunger and thirst) and to the preservation of the species (termed sexual drives). In *Beyond the Pleasure Principle* (1920) he grouped these drives together, calling them Eros or life drives. At this point he posited an additional set of drives that were antagonistic to Eros. He named these the aggressive or death drives (Thanatos), as their aim was to move towards extinction – the equivalent in personal terms perhaps of the 'heat-death of the universe'.

For Freud, drives had the goal of conserving an earlier state of affairs, and so the death drive embodies the tendency for living organisms to return to the inanimate state. 'The aim of all life is death . . . inanimate things existed before living ones . . .' (Freud 1920). The death drive has remained a controversial concept within the psychoanalytic world after Freud. Melanie Klein's use of this concept is discussed later in this chapter.

Freud emphasized the importance of childhood for adult functioning, particularly the first five years of life. He came to believe that the major influence on development was the psychosocial conflict surrounding the sexual drive during these early years of life. The pervasive importance of this drive in shaping development and adult functioning was seen to arise from a number of its properties.

Sexuality begins early in life and its development is long and complicated, making it very prone to distortion. Further, 'the sexual instincts are remarkable for their plasticity, for the facility with which they can change their aim . . . for the ease with which they can substitute one form of gratification for another' (Freud 1938: 127). This means that many aspects of life can be sexualized. Therefore, in addition to biological development, environment and social context exert important influences on both the form and the expression of the sexual drive.

Freud gradually evolved a model of human development described in psychosexual stages. He identified three early (pre-genital) stages of sexual development. The characteristics of infantile sexual life were considered 'essentially auto-erotic (i.e. that it finds its object in the infant's own body) and that its individual component instincts are upon the whole disconnected and independent of one another in their search for pleasure' (Freud 1905: 63).

Each stage has become known by the area of the body seen as the predominant erogenous, or 'erotogenic', zone during that particular version of the psychosexual conflict between instinctual drive and society: oral, anal and phallic.

Each erotogenic zone is associated with a vital somatic function: the oral zone with feeding, the anal zone with defecation and so on. It is through the pleasurable sensation that accompanies fulfilment of any of these somatic functions that an erotogenic zone becomes established. A need to repeat this pleasurable sensation arises, which then becomes separate from the somatic function.

Sexual development is 'diphasic', that is, it occurs in two waves. The pre-genital stages are brought to a halt, or 'retreat', by a period called 'latency'. A 'second wave sets in with puberty and determines the final outcome of sexual life' (Freud 1905: 66).

These phases of 'sexual organization' are normally passed through smoothly, with little more than a hint of their existence. 'It is only in pathological cases that they become active and recognisable to superficial observation' (Freud 1905: 64). Too little or too much gratification at any stage results in the individual becoming 'fixated'. Freud described how, at times of stress throughout life, such 'fixation points' could be pre-dispositional. The precise impact would vary according to what stage frustration or indulgence happened and what form it took.

Each stage therefore has an adult character type associated with it and particular defences which predominate. These defences become particularly strong if fixation occurs. The character traits related to fixation at any stage are described in terms of bipolar opposites, either of which may be shown, although there is of course here something of a 'heads I win, tails you lose' argument, in as much as anal fixation, for example, can be interpreted in terms of extreme tidiness or extreme messiness.

Freud came to believe that the three pre-genital stages did not succeed each other in a clear-cut fashion: 'one may appear in addition to another; they may overlap one another, may be present alongside of one another' (Freud 1940: 155). He also outlined how much from each earlier stage, 'obtains permanent representation in the economy of the libido and in the character of the individual' (Freud 1938: 130).

The oral stage (the first year of life)

Freud describes how the first organ to emerge as an erotogenic zone is the mouth, through the action of sucking.

> To begin with, all psychical activity is concentrated on providing satisfaction for the needs of that zone. Primarily, of course, this satisfaction serves the purpose of self-preservation by means of nourishment; . . . The baby's obstinate persistence in sucking gives evidence . . . of a need for satisfaction which, though it originates from and is instigated by the taking of nourishment, nevertheless strives to obtain pleasure independently of nourishment and for that reason may and should be termed *sexual*.
>
> (Freud 1940: 154)

Sensual sucking is described as rhythmic and as 'not infrequently combined with rubbing some sensitive part of the body such as the breast or the external genitalia. Many children proceed by this path from sucking to masturbation' (Freud 1905: 46).

He points out how during the oral, or 'cannibalistic', stage, 'sexual activity has not yet been separated from the ingestion of food . . . The sexual aim is incorporation of the object – the prototype of a process which, in the form of identification, is later to play such an important psychological part' (Freud 1905: 64).

> So the infant seeks to take in or incorporate whatever he comes across or experiences. At this stage his well being is largely dependent on others. If his needs are satisfied, he comes to conceive of existence in a positive way and to see the world about him as warm and benevolent. If he is deprived, his emotional orientation may well be pessimistic; he comes to anticipate that the world will be unrewarding and hostile to his needs . . . fixation at this stage . . . is likely to result in an adult who is overly concerned with oral gratification.
>
> (Stevens 1983a: 40)

The potential conflicts at this stage are therefore around taking and receiving. Receiving represents the earliest, passive experience of the infant being given nourishment, and taking the more active attempts by the infant to satisfy oral needs by mouthing and sucking objects. There are three main defences of the oral stage, all of which are a part of normal development: denial, projection and introjection (see the companion volume in this series on *Defences and Resistance*, Davy and Cross, forthcoming). Freud describes how, 'during this oral phase sadistic impulses already occur sporadically along with the appearance of teeth' (Freud 1940: 154). More needs to be said about this aspect when discussing Karl Abraham's elaborations on the psychosexual stages.

The anal stage (1 to 3 years old)

'Like the labial zone, the anal zone is well suited by its position to act as a medium through which sexuality may attach itself to other somatic functions.' Freud (1905: 51) During the infant's second year, physical development enables the beginnings of bowel control. This leads to a shift of the erotogenic zone to the anus, as the contents of the bowels act 'as a stimulating mass upon a sexually sensitive portion of mucous membrane' (Freud 1905: 52). The sexual drive becomes centred around the pleasurable sensations of expelling or retaining faeces. As a consequence of this physical development, caregivers' expectations for continence also increase. Personality development is greatly influenced by how this experience of toilet training is handled.

Freud describes how, in this 'sadistic-anal' organization, the opposition between two currents, one active and one passive, which run through all sexual life, is already developed. 'The activity is put into operation by the instinct for mastery through the agency of the somatic musculature; the organ which, more than any other, represents the passive sexual aim is the erotogenic mucous membrane of the anus.' (Freud 1905: 64) So mastery of the bodily musculature during this stage ushers forth 'auto-erotic' pleasurable sensations accompanying the expelling or retaining of faeces. It also enables the child to begin to delay gratification in order to please others, or attempt to control caregivers by withholding or expelling faeces inappropriately. Potential conflicts are concerned with giving (anal expulsiveness) and withholding (anal retentiveness). Social conditioning really comes to the fore during this stage. Parental disgust at the child who gets toilet training wrong may lead to shame and guilt; parental praise for using the potty and being 'clean' may elicit pride.

The infant regards their faeces as part of their own body; faeces represent an infant's first 'gift'. By producing faeces 'he can express his active compliance with his environment and by withholding them, his disobedience' (Freud 1905: 52).

Therefore, this stage is seen as the beginning of a shift in drives, from being purely auto-erotic to having objects – a significant development not just in child development but also in Freud's theory, representing the first hint of the move from drive theory to object relations theory. Freud describes an intermediate phase between the auto-erotic and object relating, which he called (healthy) 'narcissism'. Unlike in auto-eroticism, at this point the infant has a concept of her own person; so the infant's own body comes to be the sexual object – she loves herself as herself. As Rycroft (1972: 72) notes, Freud further differentiated between '*primary narcissism*, the love of self which precedes loving others, and *secondary narcissism*, love of self which results from introjecting and identifying with an object.' Confusingly, in psychoanalytic writing the term 'narcissism' has subsequently been used to describe many different concepts.

The anal stage is also the beginning of 'ambivalence', as the active and passive currents are almost equally developed. Sadistic impulses begin to act to a greater extent. These are seen as a 'fusion of purely libidinal and purely destructive urges' (Freud 1940: 154). However, one of the things that characterizes these early pre-genital stages remains that 'the combination of the component instincts and their subordination under the primacy of the genitals have been effected only very incompletely or not at all' (Freud 1905: 65).

In the *Three Essays on Sexuality* (1905) Freud makes it clear that although the focus at this stage is on the musculature involved in defecation there is also sexual pleasure in muscular activity generally: 'children feel the need for a large amount of muscular exercise and derive extraordinary pleasure from satisfying it' (Freud 1905: 68).

> In response to the demands made upon him, he can submit, rebel or learn to cope with authority while maintaining his own autonomy . . . if the pleasure a child takes in playing with his faeces is severely constrained by his parents, for example, he may develop defences against such forbidden pleasures which may express themselves later as obsessive orderliness and cleanliness. If parents reinforce his production on the potty, this may lay the foundation for later pleasure in creating. And miserliness may result from a child developing an unwillingness to 'let go'.
>
> (Stevens 1983: 41)

The predominant defences related to this stage are 'isolation', 'intellectualization', 'reaction formation' and 'undoing'.

The phallic stage (3 to 6 years old)

At around the age of 3 years the predominant erogenous zone is thought to shift to the genitalia as children begin to explore their own and others' bodies. The area of the genitals is stimulated in the course of everyday washing and drying, and the child learns to stimulate this area for themselves.

Freud's theorizing about this stage shifted several times as his ideas developed. Early on he posited that the anal organization was followed by the genital. Later he reformulated this position, clarifying that it was not the genitals but the phallus that predominated. 'It is to be noted that it is not the genitals of both sexes that play a part at this stage but only the male ones (the phallus). The female genitals long remain unknown' (Freud 1940: 154). At this point in his thinking Freud viewed the development of both genders to be related to the norm of male sexuality. '*Maleness* exists, but not *femaleness*. The antithesis here is between having *a male genital* and being *castrated*. It is not until development has reached its completion at puberty that the sexual polarity coincides with male and female' (Freud 1923: 312, Freud's italics). Jacobs (1992: 48) highlights how this position seemed to shift again in Freud's last papers.

Although he appears in places to hold to identical development in boys and girls in the pre-genital stages (1933a: 151), he made a significant recognition of the way girls and boys differ in their earliest relationships, for example pre-Oedipal exclusive attachment to mothers is greater in women than men (1931b: 377).

The phallic stage is seen as a 'forerunner of the final form taken by sexual life' (Freud 1940: 154). The child's curiosity about sexual differences becomes heightened, 'the sexuality of early childhood reaches its height and approaches its dissolution' (Freud 1940: 154). Freud (1940) suggests that both boys and girls, 'have begun to put their intellectual activity at the service of sexual researches', and that both 'start off from the premise of the universal presence of the penis'. From this point the paths of the sexes begin to diverge. The boy initially views the girl's clitoris as an even smaller penis than his own and then moves on to believe that the little girl has been castrated.

This gives rise to the boy's own fear of castration. The girl, 'comes to recognise her lack of a penis or rather the inferiority of her clitoris, with permanent effects on the development of her character; as a result of this first disappointment in rivalry, she often begins by turning away altogether from sexual life' (Freud 1940: 155). Freud acknowledged that he was more confident about describing male development.

This concern with sexual differences is played out in the phallic stage through 'the central phenomenon of the sexual period of early childhood' (Freud 1924: 315) – a conflict that Freud eventually named the Oedipus complex. Put at its most simple, the child is believed to develop incestuous desires for the parent of the opposite sex along with the desire to displace the same-sex parent. Freud sees resolution of this Oedipal conflict as the key to successful psychosexual development. Wolheim (1971: 120) describes the male child's passage through this conflict, including the rather more complex picture that Freud in fact posits:

> On account of the loving wish for the mother and the hostile wish against the father, the child feels itself threatened by the father, and this threat is represented in the mind as the threat of castration. The child, however, also loves his father; and so along with fear of the father goes some measure of fear for the father – fear, that is for the father on account of his, the child's, hostility. In consequence of these two fears, the child's sexuality comes to grief and is altogether suppressed: and the so-called latency period sets in.

So the objects that are both desired and feared are given up and become replaced with identifications that are formative in later sex role behaviour. This also leads to the introjection of parental attitudes and the beginnings of the superego or conscience. Freud's description of female psychosexual development at this stage is both less clear and more controversial. Freud initially assumed that girls followed a parallel development to that of boys through the Oedipal conflict. Later he came to view as a key experience the little girl's realization that neither she, her mother, nor any woman has a penis. Freud describes how this gives rise to penis envy and the little girl's devaluing of all women. 'She has seen it and knows that she is without it and wants to have it . . . After a woman has become aware of the wound to her narcissism, she develops, like a scar, a sense of inferiority' (Freud 1925b: 336, 337). For this she blames her mother 'who sent her into the world insufficiently equipped' (Freud 1925b: 338). The girl gives up her wish for a penis, substituting a wish for a child and thus shifting her interest to her father as love-object. So for girls the Oedipus complex is not really resolved, and according to Freud this means that the superego is less well developed. (See Gilligan in chapter 5 for a full critique of this suggestion.)

Jacobs (1992: 150) describes how 'actual sexual abuse, or even emotional seduction of children, or the use of children by parents as allies in their own warring relationship, . . . makes the possibility of resolution of the Oedipus complex much more difficult'. Jacobs acknowledges Freud's much-criticized shift from stories of actual seduction to a belief that neuroses more frequently resulted from phantasies of seduction. He also points out that Freud did not completely retract his belief in actual seduction.

According to Freud, in the earlier pre-genital stages 'the different component instincts set about their pursuit of pleasure independently of one another; in the phallic phase there are the beginnings of an organisation which subordinates the other urges to the primacy of the genitals and signifies the start of a co-ordination of the general urge towards pleasure into the sexual function' (1940: 155). The main defence of the phallic stage is repression; that is, avoiding the anxiety aroused by instinctual wishes by pushing them out of awareness.

The latency stage (6 years of age to puberty)

Latency follows the resolution of the Oedipus complex in boys – or the equivalent and different shift Freud thought occurred in girls. It is a time of relative dormancy of the sexual drive and consequently of a reduction in conflict. The term 'latency' is not intended to imply that sexual impulses are absent, but rather that the child can focus more on the external and social world, freed from some of the interference of concerns from the previous stages. Sexual energy is diverted into affection, acting as a transitional stage in the development of loving relationships at adolescence. Jacobs (1992: 48–9) points out that, 'although Freud said that this period was culturally determined, "a product of education", he also felt that the development "is organically determined and fixed by heredity"'. It was viewed as essential to the development of advanced civilization, as well as playing a significant part in the predisposition to neuroses through the action of disgust and shame.

The genital stage (from puberty onwards)

At puberty the physical development of the sexual system is completed and sexual feelings re-emerge. They are no longer self-directed
(auto-erotic) but now involve seeking an object, eventually perhaps a
partner. The genital stage represents the completion of development,
the attainment of mature sexuality combining the learning from all
the earlier pre-genital stages. Sensual and affectionate expression
merge, and the natural aim of the sexual drive is now genital sexual
intercourse. Freud describes the complete organization as

a state of things . . . in which

(1) some earlier libidinal cathexes are retained,
(2) others are taken into the sexual function as preparatory,
    auxiliary acts, the satisfaction of which produces what is
    known as fore-pleasure, and
(3) other urges are excluded from the organisation, and are
    either suppressed altogether (repressed) or are employed in
    the ego in another way, forming character-traits or undergo-
    ing sublimation with a displacement of their aims.

(Freud 1940: 155)

Though the genital character is socially well adjusted, because
expression of the sexual instinct continues to be subject to societal
expectations, even mature genital functioning is not free of some
conflict requiring a defensive response. The major defence of the
genital stage is sublimation. In sublimation, instinctual drives are
given expression in a more socially acceptable form, thus being successfully discharged. This is also known as aim-inhibited sexuality or
love.

Karl Abraham on psychosexual stages

Karl Abraham, one of Freud's earliest followers and colleagues,
expanded upon the psychosexual stages, notably in *A Short Study of
the Development of the Libido, Viewed in the Light of Mental Disorders*
(1924).

A major contribution to the stage model was the subdivision of
oral, anal and genital stages, which, as outlined by Symington, are as
follows:

1. Earlier oral stage – auto-erotism, pre-ambivalent
2. Later oral stage – narcissism, oral-sadistic
3. Earlier anal-sadistic stage – partial love with incorporation
4. Later anal sadistic stage – partial love
5. Earlier genital stage – object love with exclusion of genitals
6. Later genital stage – object love

(Symington 1986: 158)

Abraham was both the first psychoanalyst to focus upon character formation and the first to attend to the importance of the child's early relationship with its mother, or more specifically its mother's breast. In many ways he presages the ideas developed by Melanie Klein – not surprisingly since he was her second analyst. Freud acknowledged Abraham's new subdivisions in the *New Introductory Lectures on Psychoanalysis* (1938: 129), beginning with the oral stage. 'In the earlier stage of it we only have oral incorporation, and there is no ambivalence in the relation to the object, i.e. the mother's breast. The second stage, which is distinguished by the onset of biting activities, may be called the "oral-sadistic" stage. It is here that we get the first manifestations of ambivalence.' So in the earlier oral stage the child cannot distinguish between itself and its mother, much as Winnicott was later to suggest. Symington (1986: 161–2) describes how for Abraham, the infant's 'pleasure in sucking gets transferred to the anal and urethral sphincters' . . . so . . . 'pleasure in soiling or retention of faeces, therefore, can be a response to overindulgence at the oral stage. That is, anal traits develop from the ruins of an oral eroticism whose development has miscarried.'

Abraham subdivided the anal stage into earlier and later stages in an attempt to account for the development of melancholia and obsessional neuroses.

In the former of these the destructive tendencies to annihilate and to get rid of things have the upper hand, while in the latter those tendencies predominate which are friendly to the object, and seek to possess things and hold them fast. In the middle of this phase, then, there appears for the first time a consideration for the object, which is a forerunner of a later relation of love towards the object.

(Freud 1938: 129)

Though Abraham sought only to expand upon Freud's stages of development, he did differ from him in his view of the relationship between the individual and society. Whereas Freud believed that there was an inevitable opposition between the two, Abraham believed that, in mature man, the needs of the individual and society could come together.

Anna Freud and ego psychology

In the *Three Essays on the Theory of Sexuality* (1905: 73), Freud describes puberty as the time when 'changes set in which are destined to give infantile sexual life its final normal shape'. Anna Freud, his daughter, became particularly interested in the period of adolescence and extended Freud's developmental theory to expand upon what takes place during this time.

Where Freud had worked mostly with adults and concentrated his attention on id impulses and the unconscious elements of intra-psychic life, Anna Freud worked with children and adolescents and was more interested in the place of the ego in the dynamics of the psyche. That focus on ego became known as ego psychology. Erik Erikson, whose ideas are explored in chapter two, is perhaps the best-known exponent of ego psychology, and was certainly strongly influenced by Anna Freud's ideas on adolescence through his training with her. Another important exponent of ego psychology is Heinz Hartmann.

Anna Freud based her ideas upon child observation as well as her extensive analytic work with children and adolescents. She described how the physical changes of adolescence were accompanied by an increase in impulses such as the sexual drive. An imbalance between id and ego resulted. Adolescence was, therefore, 'by its nature an interruption to peaceful growth . . . it is normal for an adolescent to behave for a considerable length of time in an inconsistent and unpredictable manner' (A. Freud 1998: 195–6). She considers these fluctuations between extremes to be signs of normal development, 'no more than the adult structure of personality taking a long time to emerge' (A. Freud 1998: 196). It is instead the 'one-sided suppression, or revolt, or flight, or withdrawal, or regression, or asceticism, which are responsible for the truly pathological developments' (A. Freud 1998: 196). Adolescence was seen as a time of great uncertainty about the self. Issues of self-identity subconsciously come to pervade every-thing that is done. To regain psychological equilibrium the adolescent is faced with the task of balancing the instinctual wishes of the id against the social demands of the ego.

Another of Anna Freud's major contributions to developmental theory is the idea of viewing any given child against the background of a developmental norm. Such norms are described as 'developmental lines' (A. Freud 1963). They 'trace the child's gradual outgrowing of dependent, irrational, id- and object-determined attitudes to an increasing ego mastery of his internal and external world' (A. Freud 1963: 245). For example, the line from the body to the toy and from play to work. Play begins with the child's first erotic pleasure from the mother's body. This role is transferred to the first soft plaything, the 'transitional object' (Winnicott 1953), gradually broadening to other toys and then to games more generally. As direct satisfaction from the play activity slowly gives way to pleasure in the finished product and impulse control develops, ability to play changes into ability to work.

Object relations theory

Sigmund Freud originally appears to have believed that the only value of interactions with other people was the part that they could play in satisfying instincts. Object relations theorists believe that interactions with others are more than merely an outcome of attempts to maximize instinctual gratification. The mechanistic-sounding term 'object' came from Freud's own use of it in relation to instincts having a source, an aim and an 'object', literally referring to whatever is the target or satisfaction of a need. Objects can be people, parts of a person (like the mother's breast) or a non-human article of attachment.

There is not one central theorist who can be seen as responsible for the theory of personality development described as object relations theory; rather a variety of independent but related theories have emerged. Variants on object relations theory have in common the value they put on the role of interpersonal relations in personality development. Broadly, this theory views personality as being shaped by the specifics (real and perceived – the latter called phantasy) of interpersonal encounters. Through experiences of interacting with others, external relationships are taken in to become parts of we, termed 'internal objects' (Fairbairn 1954). These interactions become the building blocks of 'self-structure' (Kohut 1971), while distortions or deficits in this internalized self-structure may lead to later problems.

Melanie Klein was among the early object relations theorists, together with W.R.D. Fairbairn, Donald Winnicott and Michael Balint and others: their ideas have come to be known as the British School.

Similar theories developed in the USA, with analysts such as Harry Stack Sullivan, Erich Fromm, Karen Horney, Frieda Fromm-Reichmann and others becoming known as interpersonal psychoanalysts.

These theorists were originally trained in psychoanalysis, and many of them have sought to maintain coherence with this tradition, even if some left the mainstream institutions and founded schools of their own. They have viewed object relations as an addition to Freud's theorizing rather than as a replacement for it. Others, notably Otto Kernberg, while remaining within institutionalized psychoanalysis have seen their underlying assumptions about development as irreconcilable and have defined themselves as separate. Michael Kahn (1991) makes a case for the usefulness of both approaches, seeing Freud's theories as helpful for understanding internal intra-psychic development and object relations theory as helpful for understanding interpersonal development.

Melanie Klein

Melanie Klein, like Anna Freud, although in a different country and developing in a different direction both in theory and technique, pioneered the use of therapy with children through play. Through observations of children she came to believe that they were more occupied with the need to manage feelings directed towards the central figures around them than with the erotic impulses on which Freud had focused. She saw the mother–child relationship as central in personality development, forming a sort of prototype for all other relationships; and she believed that intra-psychic development in a child's first year of life dictated much of later personality. This emphasis on the first year (as, for example, the time of the Oedipus complex, first feelings of guilt, and so on) distinguishes her model from that of Freud, in which the first five years are significant.

Klein's developmental theory remained compatible with Freud's in acknowledging the motivating role played by instinctual drives. In fact Klein reformulates Freud's death instinct (Thanatos), putting the emphasis on aggressive impulses rather than on impulses towards self-extinction. The conflict between the instinctual forces of life and death, for Klein, is projected out on to objects in the external world.

Klein suggests that a newborn infant has an ego already able to feel anxiety, make use of defences and begin to form object relations in phantasy and reality. For Klein, it is through this ongoing process of introjection and projection of objects rather than through the Freudian psychosexual stages that the ego develops. From birth the infant exists in relation to another person, or part of a person (a part-object), beginning with the mother, and more particularly with the mother's breast, as the primary object. The breast is experienced at times as satisfying and ideal, and at other times as frustrating or persecutory. It is the infant's own aggressive impulses that give rise to these persecutory feelings about the breast.

Klein's developmental theory emphasizes the role of innate ambivalence and phantasy in early development. Ambivalence arises from the innate conflict between the instinctual drives of life and death that are manifested as love and hate, destructiveness and envy. From birth the infant tries to manage this tension by 'bringing them together in order to modify the death drive with the life drive or by expelling the death drive into the outside world' (Mitchell 1986: 19). Klein sees resolution of this innate tension towards mother and breast as central within the development of personality, through holding together conflicting feelings and conflicting perceptions of the other – this holding together being known as ambivalence. The infant's *actual* experience of mothering is given less emphasis, while the relation to parental objects in phantasy is seen to play a central part in what is taken in (by the process of introjection) to become a part of the 'self'. It is in this aspect in particular that Klein's developmental theory markedly diverges from the object relations theories of Winnicott and Fairbairn.

Strachey has pointed out that Freud variously used two different definitions of instincts: one that implies that an instinct *is* its mental representation, and one that differentiates between the two. Klein uses the term 'phantasy' to refer to this mental expression of instincts. The archaic 'ph' spelling for fantasy is intended to indicate that the process is an unconscious one. As instincts are on the frontier between the somatic and the mental, the phantasies derived from them are also experienced as being both somatic and mental phenomena. Mitchell (1986: 23) describes how

> In Klein's concept, phantasy emanates from within and imagines what is without, it offers an unconscious commentary on instinctual life and links feelings to objects and creates a new amalgam: the world of imagination. Through its ability to phantasize the baby tests out, primitively 'thinks' about, its experiences of inside and outside. External reality can gradually affect

and modify the crude hypotheses phantasy sets up. Phantasy is both the activity and its products.

So for Klein, normal development principally involves managing the opposing inner forces of love and hate, of preservation and destruction. She replaces Freud's concept of *stages* of development with descriptions of *positions*. Her use of the term positions emphasizes that these are to be seen as 'a specific configuration of object relations, anxieties and defences which persist *throughout* life' (Segal, 1973, p. ix; our emphasis).

She describes two positions: the 'paranoid schizoid position', spanning the first 3 to 4 months of life; and the 'depressive position', which begins at about 3 to 4 months. Both positions continue to play a forceful role, to different degrees according to different circumstances, throughout childhood, adolescence and adult life. In the paranoid schizoid position, anxiety is experienced by the early infant's ego both through the internal, innate conflict between the opposing instincts for life and death (manifested as destructive envy) and by interactions in external reality. Hannah Segal describes how 'when faced with the anxiety produced by the death instinct, the ego deflects it' (Segal 1973: 25). She goes on to describe how, for Klein this deflection

> consists partly of a projection, partly of the conversion of the death instinct into aggression. The ego splits itself and projects that part of itself, which contains the death instinct outwards into the original external object – the breast. Thus, the breast, which is felt to contain a great part of the infant's death instinct, is felt to be bad and threatening to the ego, giving rise to a feeling of persecution. In that way, the original fear of the death instinct is changed into fear of a persecutor.

The remainder of the death instinct within the self is transformed to aggression aimed at this persecutor. A similar process of projection onto the breast occurs with the life instinct, creating a 'good' (or gratifying) object.

So from early on the ego comes to relate to the primary object of the mother's breast as 'split' into two parts: a 'good', pleasurable and 'ideal' part; and a 'bad', frustrating and 'persecutory' part.

This paranoid schizoid position is characterized by persecutory anxiety, with the infant fearing annihilation by the bad object, thus the term 'paranoid'; and by maintenance of a relationship with the 'good' object, through phantasized splitting of the infant ego, emphasized by the term 'schizoid'. The infant ego does not yet have the ability to tolerate or integrate these different aspects, and thus makes use of magical omnipotent denial in order to remove the power and reality from the persecutory object, and manage these inner impulses.

The depressive position, a curious term that has little to do with depression, describes integration. It represents a significant step in development occurring with the infant's discovery that the hated breast and the loved breast are one and the same. Mother begins to be recognized as a whole object who can be good and bad, rather than two part-objects, one good and one bad. Love and hate, along with external reality and intra-psychic reality (phantasy), can also begin to co-exist.

With the acceptance of ambivalence, mother begins to be seen as fallible and capable of good and bad, and the infant begins to acknowledge its own helplessness, dependency and jealousy towards the mother. The child becomes anxious that their aggressive impulses have harmed or even destroyed the mother, whom they now recognize as needed and loved. This results in 'depressive anxiety' replacing destructive urges with guilt.

W.R.D. Fairbairn

Fairbairn's theory was perhaps the first fully 'relational' theory of development. He viewed people as social beings who are primarily motivated, not by sexual or aggressive drives, but in seeking out satisfying relationships with others. So they are primarily 'object seeking'. In contrast to Klein's emphasis on the infant's phantasies. it is real interaction with caregivers that has the greatest importance for development according to Fairbairn.

Fairbairn's developmental theory, like that of Klein, emphasizes the role played by the early relationship between mother and child. He goes into further detail about a range of 'object relations', drops the term id, and although he retains the traditional psychoanalytic terms of ego and libido, confusingly he uses these terms differently. Like Klein, he believed that infants are born with a functional ego. However, for Fairbairn, it is the ego that is the source of libido, not the impersonal id. Libido is an energy of desire for emotional contact. The erotogenic zones (mouth, anus, penis and vagina) are merely the pathway to this contact with the object.

Fairbairn bases his developmental terms around the issue of

dependence within the infant's early relationships. He describes three developmental phases: 'infantile dependence', 'quasi-independence' and 'mature dependence'. The first phase, infantile dependence, is marked by little differentiation between mother and child. Fairbairn describes this near fusion as a state of 'primary identification'. The second phase of 'quasi-independence' is a long 'transitional stage'. It entails the continuing organization of the internal world into more clearly differentiated representations of objects. This phase is characterized by discrimination, acceptance and rejection. Mature dependence, the final phase, might more accurately be described as mature interdependence, as it is marked by mutuality and cooperation between equals. In relationships at this 'mature' phase of development, difference and underlying healthy dependency can both be acknowledged.

For Fairbairn, the transition from dependence to interdependence continues throughout life, and problems of development arise from difficulties in negotiating these transitions and separations. Fairbairn believes that the psychoneuroses associated with pathology in Freud's model of the psychosexual stages are normative, defensive techniques of the transitional stage ('transitional stage techniques'). He believes that they help the child towards greater object differentiation. If these techniques persist into later life they do become pathological, showing as phobic, hysteric, obsessional or paranoid behaviour.

At birth the infant has a non-ambivalent and totally dependent relationship towards the mother (breast). Experiences of frustration and rejection are an inevitable part of this relationship and because of dependency, the infant can neither control mother nor abandon her. Fairbairn suggests that this results in the infant splitting the mother into good and bad aspects, which can then be kept apart from one another psychologically and thus allow necessary dependence to continue.

'The infant's inner world is split into "good" and "bad" internal objects as a defensive measure adopted by the child to deal with his original object (the mother and her breast) in so far as it is unsatisfying.' (Fairbairn 1963). The inner representative of the comforting and satisfying mother, the 'good' internalized object, is called the 'ego ideal' or 'ideal object'. This is the source of the child's feeling of being desirable and loved. The 'bad' or 'unsatisfying' internalized objects are conceptualized as two separate aspects: either as 'exciting objects', stemming from maternal interactions that are tantalizing and over-stimulating; or 'frustrating objects', which arise from maternal interactions that are withholding or rejecting.

Through the action of splitting and repression of these parts, the child's ego is split into three ego states: a 'central (conscious) ego' deriving from the ideal object (ego ideal); a repressed, 'libidinal ego', associated with the exciting (libidinal) object; and a repressed 'anti-libidinal ego' associated with the rejecting (or anti-libidinal) object. Fairbairn calls this internal situation the schizoid position, although this is different from the paranoid schizoid position described by Klein.

Children dominated by the libidinal ego state feel empty, deprived and frustrated. Those dominated by the anti-libidinal ego state feel chronic rage and, though they yearn for acceptance, feel unloved and unlovable. So, problems in development arise from these extremes of splitting and repression.

D.W. Winnicott

Winnicott was influenced early on by Melanie Klein, although he differs from her in a number of significant ways, including, like Fairbairn, the emphasis on the actual, experienced, relational environment for development rather than on phantasy and the innate. He conceives of a 'natural' growth towards maturity that depends upon the provision of a 'good-enough facilitating environment' (1971: 139) and describes development as three progressive phases: absolute dependence, relative dependence and towards independence.

The infant's absolute dependence in the first few weeks after birth is met by what Winnicott describes as 'primary maternal preoccupation' (Winnicott 1956). This is a heightened sense of awareness in the mother about herself and her baby that enables her to respond to the child with perfect attunement. Ego development thus depends upon the mother providing 'good-enough ego-coverage' to help contain the baby's 'unthinkable anxieties':

1. going to pieces;
2. falling for ever;
3. having no relationship to the body;
4. having no orientation; and
5. complete isolation because of there being no means of communication.

(1965: 58)

During this time, mother and child are seen as merged, existing in a state of 'seamless oneness' (Winnicott 1960a). The infant is hungry, and when the breast appears, the infant experiences itself as omnipotent, as having itself created the breast. Hazler and Barwick (2001: 32), in a companion volume in this series, describe how the mother 'plays the role of supportive ego, sustaining the baby's omnipotent illusion'. Winnicott regards this infantile illusion of omnipotence as an ordinary and necessary aspect of child development. He believes that such healthy development of the 'true self' (the inherited disposition of the child) occurs in an atmosphere of acceptance and care, with a caregiver who is attuned and responsive to the child's 'spontaneous gestures'. Such a 'good-enough mother' (Winnicott 1954) offers at the 'right time', rather than imposing her own timing and needs; and, in this way, provides a 'good-enough' 'holding environment' with an optimum amount of constancy and comfort. With sufficient experiences of responsive maternal attunement, the infant builds the security needed to begin to tolerate inevitable failures of empathy. The maternal 'holding' environment provides stability and constancy, literally a sort of holding together of the infant, a sense of 'going on being'.

The shift to the next phase, relative dependence, is distinguished from the first phase as a state 'that the infant can know about' (1965: 87); that is, the child begins to gain an awareness of their dependence, and through experiencing mother's absence, also learns about loss.

This process occurs as the mother's adaptation to her child gradually begins to lessen and small environmental 'failures' begin to occur. These maternal failures, described by Winnicott (1960a) as 'impingements', if occurring in well-timed 'small doses', help the child to learn that they are not omnipotent and encourage a sense of separateness. So during relative dependence the mother functions as a sort of buffer between the child and the outside world. Her 'failure' to adapt helps the child to adapt to external reality, and the child's developing intellect enables toleration of maternal failures in adaptation. 'In this way the mind is allied to the mother and takes over part of her function' (1965: 7). But, as Hazler and Barwick (2001: 32) describe, if 'impingements occur too early or are too intense, the infant's experience is not of a loosening hold but of being "dropped" '.

This task of 'disillusionment' is again an important part of normal development. As the infant gradually begins to be able to differentiate itself from its mother, the capacity to form symbols develops. Winnicott describes how this time between merger and separation is bridged through the action of a 'transitional object'. This is the infant's first 'not-me' possession, often a blanket or toy with a characteristic feel and smell. It acts to provide the comfort of mother when she is not available and thus promotes separation and autonomy.

The third phase of development, towards independence, 'is never absolute. The healthy individual does not become isolated, but becomes related to the environment in such a way that the individual and the environment can be said to be interdependent' (1965: 84).

Like Anna Freud, Winnicott considers the parent/child conflicts of adolescence to be important developmentally. Jacobs (1995: 45), quoting Winnicott, describes how,

> for healthy development the adolescent needs 'to avoid the false solution . . . to feel real or to tolerate not feeling at all . . . to defy in a setting in which dependence is met and can be relied on to be met . . . to prod society repeatedly so that society's antagonism is made manifest, and can be met with antagonism'.
>
> (1965: 85)

Jacobs (1995: 55) goes on to describe how adolescents

> have to discover their own maturation, which includes their need to challenge and metaphorically to kill off their parents. Parents cannot make this happen. They 'can help only a little: the best they can do is to *survive*, to survive intact, and without changing colour, without relinquishment of any important 'principle' (1971: 145, Winnicott's italics).

Margaret Mahler

Margaret Mahler was a paediatrician. Through her work with autistic and psychotic children she began to focus on bonding and interruptions in the early mother and child relationship. She developed a theory of personality based around the process of separating and differentiating the self from others. The course of this early separation process is seen as setting the template for future relationships with others. It is the beginning of a life-long process of 'separation-differentiation'.

A number of phases in the development of the self are identified, from psychological fusion to separation. These phases concentrate on mother and child interactions over the first three years of life. Mahler (1968) terms them the 'autistic phase', the 'symbiotic phase' and the 'separation-individuation phase', the last of which is made up of a series of sub-phases. These phases overlap each other, and the final phase, separation-individuation, is the beginning of a process that continues throughout life.

The first phase, 'normal autism', occupies the child's first 3 to 4 weeks. The infant is unaware of other people during this time, responding only to bodily tensions. Fixation at this stage may be responsible for the most extreme psychotic states in adulthood.

At the age of 2 to 3 months, vague awareness begins of a link between the mother (or the primary caregiver) and tension reduction. This is the beginning of the symbiotic phase. Though there is some awareness of mother, she is not yet perceived as separate. The infant continues to need the mother's close emotional attunement, but failures during this phase may also lead to psychoses in adulthood.

From around 5 months to about 3 to 4 years old, the most involved stage, separation-individuation, takes place. Interaction during this phase is crucial in laying down the development of the sense of self and manner of relating to others taken on into adulthood. Mahler breaks this stage into four sub-phases: differentiation, practising, rapprochement and libidinal object constancy (Mahler *et al.* 1975). Each of these sub-phases is broadly linked to advances in the child's physical development.

The differentiation sub-phase occurs from approximately 5 months through to 10 months. This is prompted by the child's improving visual and sensory abilities; the mother begins to be experienced as separate. During this time 'stranger anxiety' emerges.

As the child gains sufficient physical ability to crawl, at around 10 or 11 months, the practising sub-phase takes over. For the first time the child has the ability to physically distance themselves from mother. Mahler describes this as the time of the child's 'psychological birth'. During this sub-phase the infant makes movements away from mother and continually looks to her for reassurance and 'emotional refuelling'.

As the child approaches about a year and a half, and with the beginnings of speech, feelings of self-assertion and separation come to dominate. This is the sub-phase of rapprochement. Mahler describes the rapprochement crisis in familiar terms as the obstinate battles of the 'terrible twos'. The child struggles with the increasing wish to be separate and the continuing need for reassurance and support. As Cashdan (1988: 15) writes, 'the mother's ability to successfully provide the child with the right balance of emotional support and firmness, while still allowing the child to engage in a healthy level of independent activity, is an important factor in the resolution of the crisis.'

The important final sub-phase, libidinal object constancy, takes place at around 2½ to 3 years of age. As the name implies, this sub-phase is concerned with the child gaining a stable, internal representation of the mother that can be invoked in her absence. Once able to do this, the child is enabled to function autonomously and establish healthy object relations. For libidinal object constancy to be achieved, positive and negative maternal introjects have to be integrated. Cashdan (1988: 15) describes how, if this task remains incomplete, 'the child – and later the adult – responds to those in his interpersonal environment either as punitive and rejecting or as unrealistically gratifying'. Narcissistic and borderline personality structure may result from failures during this separation-individuation phase.

Heinz Kohut

Heinz Kohut built his developmental ideas from his work with people who had narcissistic personality disorders. The focus of what he terms self psychology is on how a coherent and stable concept of self is created and maintained through early interaction with others.

He describes how from birth the child has needs for a psychological relationship in addition to physical needs. Kohut calls these needs 'normal narcissistic needs' and elaborates three different aspects that must be adequately met for normal development to proceed.

These needs are for an adequately 'mirroring', confirming response; the need to 'idealize', or merge with a calm, soothing, idealized other; and the need to feel a sense of belonging and of being like others (the alter ego need). If these are sufficiently responded to, a sense of 'self' develops, which in a healthy person functions throughout life. Kohut (1978) describes how 'the self is part of the personality that is cohesive in space, enduring in time, the centre of initiative and the recipient of impressions.'

These needs, known as 'self-object needs', begin for the infant with the 'grandiose-exhibitionistic', or mirroring, need. For this need to be adequately met, children need to receive a sufficiently strong message of their parents' delight in them.

The second essential self-object need is the idealizing need, described by Kohut as the need for an 'idealized parental imago' (1978). If the child gains sufficient experiences of perceiving one or more of their caregivers as strong, calm and capable then this need will be adequately met.

The third self-object need for the developing infant is the need to be like others, what Kohut calls the 'alter ego', or 'twinship', need. Children need to feel that they are like their carers. When this need is adequately responded to it helps to provide a feeling of belonging.

Kohut (1971) suggests that healthy development occurs when both 'gratification' and 'frustration' are optimal. There will, inevitably, be occasions when caregivers fail to provide the responses to an aspect of these needs. If these occurrences are not too traumatic and happen within a climate of adequate response on many previous occasions, these 'failures' can act as developmental opportunities.

In such circumstances, the child discovers the ability to momentarily take on each of these 'self-object' (Kohut 1978) functions for themselves. This process of external object relations becoming an inner relational structure is known as 'transmuting internalization'. Such experiences encourage the development of the child's confidence about coping with the external world and with internal conflicts and pressures. They gradually build important aspects of a strong, cohesive self.

So children who have been well 'mirrored' begin to know through such 'optimal frustrations' that they are acceptable, and are less concerned with eliciting confirmation of this from others. Children whose idealizing needs have repeatedly been well responded to begin to feel confident about their own ability to cope with both the external world and with internal conflicts and pressures; they develop the capacity to be 'self-soothing'. Children whose needs to be like others have been well met develop a sense of belonging and communal status. 'Self-object needs' are ongoing through life, and thus the process of building self-structure is never fully completed. New additions and modifications can continue to be made throughout life.

However, if a child does not receive enough positive responses in any one of these areas, the self-object need concerned may be 'traumatically frustrated'. In this event, the need begins to be denied (or in psychoanalytic terms, 'repressed', Freud, 1933) and will, therefore, remain in 'primitive' form, not becoming integrated into the self. This can lead to a variety of problems or disorders of the self in adulthood (Kohut, 1978).

So traumatic frustration of mirroring needs can result in insecurity and in lack of self-worth; it may also produce unrealistic grandiosity or boastfulness as an attempt to seek gratification of these stunted needs. Traumatic frustration of idealizing needs can lead to joylessness, and lack of vitality and inspiration; frustration of alter ego needs leads to individuals who feel somehow strange and different from other people.

There is a similarity between Winnicott's (1960a) idea of the withdrawal from authenticity and spontaneity into a 'false self' in response to a hostile world and Kohut's descriptions of problems of the self. Kohut's views on the development of the self have given rise to considerable debate and controversy, within psychoanalytic circles and beyond. Kahn (1991: 81) describes how Kohut's psychoanalytic critics viewed him as having tried to reduce the importance of sex and aggression and of softening 'the diamond hard discipline of psychoanalytic practice by introducing into it the warm softness of humanism'. Equally, Kohut's ideas have attracted supporters who view his theory as a bridge between psychodynamic and humanistic schools of thought and as providing a key framework for integration.

John Bowlby and Mary Ainsworth: attachment theory

The work of John Bowlby and Mary Ainsworth, known as attachment theory, was largely derived from parent/child observation and interview. It is an interactional model developing from the object relations approach, integrating ideas from ethnology, systems theory and cognitive psychology. A central role in development is given to intimate emotional bonds between people, called 'attachments'. Forming and maintaining these attachments is essential throughout the life cycle, but is particularly significant developmentally in the relationship between the infant and the caregiver. Attachments are 'neither subordinate to nor derivative from food and sex. . . . Instead the capacity to make intimate emotional bonds. . . . is regarded as a principal feature of effective personality functioning' (Bowlby 1998: 121).

At birth there is an array of 'developmental pathways' open to the infant. Which pathway is taken depends upon the infant's environment and particularly on interactions with the caregivers. Bowlby hypothesizes that attachment behaviour is organized by continuous feedback, a sort of interactive regulation. He views this as analogous to the physiological control systems that regulate such functions as body temperature and blood pressure; 'the attachment control system maintains a person's relation to his attachment figure between certain limits of distance and accessibility, using increasingly sophisticated methods of communication' (Bowlby 1998: 122). Attachment behaviour takes time to develop, not becoming an 'organized pattern' until the second half of the first year, as it requires the cognitive capacity to hold mother in mind when she is not present. However, from birth the infant shows a 'germinal capacity' for social interaction; and within days, by hearing, smell and by the way they are held, the infant begins to distinguish between the mother figure and other people. Bowlby describes how the building blocks for the later development of attachment are also present from birth, 'crying, sucking, clinging, and orientation. To these are added, only a few weeks later, smiling and babbling, and some months later still, crawling and walking' (1969: 319). The onset of the social smile encourages mother's attention and rapidly extends the cycles of interaction between them.

Attachment behaviour is a reciprocal relationship, with the mother figure offering responses that need to match the care-seeking behaviour of the infant. To feel attached is to feel safe and secure. This feeling of safety, known as the 'secure base' effect (Ainsworth 1982), provides a platform for curiosity, exploration and play. Proximity to the attachment figure is sought when an individual is alarmed, anxious, tired or unwell. So, 'provided the parent is known to be accessible and will be responsive when called upon, a healthy child feels secure enough to explore' (Bowlby 1998: 122).

Bowlby describes the development of attachment in four phases (1969: 319–23):

- Phase 1: orientation and signals without discrimination (circa birth to 3 months): The infant will respond to any person in the vicinity by orientation towards them, eye tracking, grasping and reaching, smiling and babbling.
- Phase 2: orientation and signals directed towards one (or more) discriminated figure(s) (circa 3 to 6 months): The infant begins to focus attention more on familiar people.
- Phase 3: maintenance of proximity to a discriminated figure by means of locomotion as well as signals (circa 6 months to 3 years): The infant actively seeks to maintain contact with the mother figure. The infant's

> repertoire of responses extends to include following a departing mother, greeting her on her return, and using her as a base from which to explore . . . the friendly and rather undiscriminating responses to everyone else wane . . . strangers become treated with increasing caution and . . . are likely to evoke alarm and withdrawal.
>
> (Bowlby 1969: 321)

- Phase 4: formation of a goal-corrected partnership (3 years and upwards): By observing the behaviour of the mother figure and what influences it, the child begins to gain insight into her feelings and motives. This ushers in a much more complex relationship between them, which Bowlby calls 'partnership'. During this phase the child increasingly tolerates separation from the mother figure and forms other close bonds.

The advent of 'stranger anxiety' during phase 3 signifies that by this time the infant has a working model of the mother figure that can be used for comparison and recognition. The infant builds such 'internal working models' of the main caregivers and their ways of communicating and behaving, along with a complimentary model of themself interacting with them. These internal working models are built from the real-life day-to-day interactions between the infant and caregivers. So what is represented in the infant's mind is 'something that has been neither entirely outside the person nor entirely inside' (Marrone 1998: 44), but rather the relationships themselves.

A securely attached child will have internal working models of reliable, responsive and loving caregivers and of a self worthy of that love. If caregivers are unpredictable or rejecting, internal working models will not be accurate representations, but will instead be built on accommodating to them.

> When a mother responds favourably only to certain of her child's emotional communications and turns a blind eye or actively discourages others, a pattern is set for the child to identify with the favoured responses and to disown the others.
>
> (Bowlby 1998: 132)

This 'coping' can take two forms, adherence or avoidance, resulting in ambivalent or avoidant attachment. (For a more in-depth description of this self-structure see the companion volume in this series by Brinich and Shelley 2002.)

Bowlby (1998: 127) describes how,

> during the first two or three years the pattern of attachment is a property of the relationship. ... if the parent treats the child differently the pattern will change accordingly. ... as a child grows older, the pattern becomes increasingly a property of the child himself, which means that he tends to impose it, or some derivative of it, upon new relationships.

As a secure child is less demanding and more rewarding to care for than an anxious child, these patterns of attachment, once established, tend to become self-perpetuating. A gradual process of updating these models occurs in healthy development so that they remain relatively contemporary representations. However, this process is impeded in anxious attachment because discrepant experience is defensively excluded. Therefore the resulting patterns of interaction continue to be imposed unchanged on whatever relationships are encountered. Opportunities for change, whether beneficial or detrimental, continue throughout life.

Holmes ((1993) 2002: 70) succinctly sums up the impact of attachment theory across the life cycle.

> For Bowlby, the human dilemma turns on the central importance of an attachment that cannot be entirely reliable, must perforce be shared, and will be lost, eventually (and often prematurely). The capacity to separate from attachment figure(s) and to form new attachments represents the developmental challenge of adolescence and young adulthood. The cycle repeats itself as parents attach themselves to their children only to let them go as *they* reach adolescence. Finally, as death of one's loved ones, and one's own death approaches, the 'monotropic' bond to life itself has gradually to be relinquished.

Daniel Stern

Stern's developmental model is based on both observation of parent–infant interaction and on his work as an adult psychoanalyst. His theory centres on the infant's changing subjective experience of self and other.

> As new behaviours and capacities emerge, they are reorganised to form organising subjective perspectives on self and other. The result is the emergence, in quantum leaps, of different senses of the self.
>
> (Stern (1985) 1998: 26)

Stern describes a sequence of 'domains of relatedness' during the first three years of life. These are not phases to be passed through. Rather, once present, each of these continues to remain active and develops throughout life.

From birth, infants begin to experience a 'sense of an emergent self'. This is the first domain. The infant is pre-designed to notice pattern and relationship, and to make connections, though they are not yet organized. Between 2 and 6 months, the 'domain of core relatedness' is built as the infant senses that they are separate from mother 'physically, are different agents, have distinct affective experiences, and have separate histories' (Stern (1985) 1998: 27). Between the 7th and 9th months of life, the 'sense of a subjective self' begins to emerge. This takes place with the infant's growing recognition that 'there are other minds out there as well as their own' (Stern (1985) 1998: 27). The 'domain of inter-subjective relatedness' thus becomes possible. The infant gains the capacity to 'attune' to mental states between people.

At around 15 to 18 months, a 'sense of verbal self' begins to emerge:

> With this new capacity for objectifying the self and co-ordinating different mental and actional schemas, infants have transcended immediate experience. They now have the psychic mechanisms and operations to share their interpersonal world knowledge and experience, as well as to work on it in imagination or reality. The advance is enormous.
>
> (Stern (1985) 1998: 167)

However, the emergence of language also causes a split in the experience of the self. We become estranged from direct contact with our own experience. As Stern succinctly puts it, 'language forces a space between interpersonal experience as lived and as represented' (Stern (1985) 1998: 182). It is in this rift that the possibility of reality distortion and neuroses arises.

Conclusions

The variety of models that have been developed within the psychoanalytic tradition demonstrates how far psychoanalytic thinking has come from the original three stages of sexuality in 1905. Drive or instinct theory has largely been replaced by object relations theory, but the models that come from infant observation still have a long way to go before they can provide any semblance of clear understanding about what this apparently crucial period of life is like in inner experience, and what effect it has on the years of childhood and adult life that follow.

The developmental theories of Erikson and Levinson

Val Simanowitz

Client Kate came to therapy in late adolescence, feeling depressed and unable to function in social settings. My impression was of a thin, wraithlike creature, colourless in both physical features and in her choice of clothing. She had just been abandoned by her boyfriend, had few friends, and felt dull and uninteresting. Whenever she tried to socialize in pubs, with groups of her peers, she found it hard to make conversation. She could not dance, so felt redundant and excluded when she accompanied her friends clubbing. As my relationship with her developed, it appeared that she was very uncertain about her identity. She had, what she described as, a dull routine job doing administration work in a computer software firm. She was an intelligent young woman who had taken herself to evening classes to do A levels (which she achieved with reasonable grades) and had interests in conservation and the environment which her friends mainly did not share. Part of her wanted to join in their funloving lifestyle, but deep down she knew she did not belong there. She had a comfortable home, living in her parents' house, but they never expressed any emotion and there was a lack of warmth. It was safe but dull. She considered it was cheap accommodation and a place where she had a considerable amount of freedom. She enjoyed the safety but part of her wanted to move away. She could not believe that she was interesting enough to be heard or that her friends, who seemed to use her as a listening ear, really valued her for herself. Erikson's ideas on identity diffusion in adolescence proved a useful framework for working with her, enabling her to become aware of the conflicting sides of herself and to some extent to reconcile them and accept them. Eventually, after a year in counselling, she took the risk of applying to university and leaving home. She

*was able to come to terms with the loss of an unhappy love relation-
ship and was seeing more of the friends who were on her wavelength.
She left therapy more confident and with a stronger sense of who she
was.*

Erik H. Erikson

One of Erikson's most significant contributions to developmental
theory is the emphasis he placed on the relationship of *society* and *the
interpersonal* to the unfolding of personality. His work is 'a change
from an activity which bases itself on a medical model as a science
applying verifiable knowledge' (Welchman 2000: 130) to one that is
more philosophical. His approach has 'a capacity to elicit meaning
and offer insights into many aspects of individual and cultural life'
(Stevens 1983b: 108).

Erikson critically examines the psychoanalytical bias towards
people's inner world (often to the exclusion of the social and political
world), and he stresses the undoubted influence of family, class and
society over the way we become fully human. Kovel describes his
model as 'a humane approach so free of analytic reductionism yet so
demonstrably enmeshed in Freudian thought' (1988: 68).

Erikson's contribution is what Stevens called a 'truly integrative
analysis'. Three main elements contribute to this integration: an
emphasis on relationship; an awareness of social and cultural context; and an insistence on the ethical foundations of psychotherapy
(Stevens 1983b: 108). Despite being steeped in Freudian concepts
of early childhood development, Erikson is able to question the
unremitting emphasis on babyhood and early childhood typical of
psychoanalysis and develop a theory that encompasses the whole
of the life cycle.

In Part 3 of *Childhood and Society* (1965) Erikson outlines what is
probably his best-known contribution to developmental theory, his
concept of life cycle development in eight distinct stages. 'In fewer
than thirty pages it embraces human life as an outline that combines
complexity with clarity, subtlety with authority, a co-ordinating
overview with a sense of immediacy and reality.' (Welchman 2000:
52) The stages are: infancy, early childhood, play age, school age,
adolescence, early adulthood, adulthood and old age.

The change from Erikson's earlier perspective is that each stage
involves *an emotional paradoxical conflict*, which needs to be confronted and resolved before the person can move on successfully to

the next stage. This conflict became the 'central feature on which all other elements converge' (Welchman 2000: 58). Erikson's insights into ego identity at the adolescent stage are particularly revealing and innovative.

Erikson's conclusions were based on research and clinical experience but were necessarily limited by his sources. In his famous essay on the development of identity in adolescence, 'The problem of ego identity' (1956), Erikson acknowledges that his sources were confined to severely disturbed young people aged between 16 and 24 who sought treatment at the clinic where he worked. He attempts to concentrate on their shared features, and acknowledges that he saw only young people who were either extremely affluent or very poor in (industrial Pittsburgh). He therefore recognizes that the middle classes were not properly represented and that most of his information was gathered from young people who were suffering mental illness at the time.

Despite this limitation, Erikson tries to offer an alternative to the current psychoanalytical focus on the 'disturbed'. Although the 'neurotic' conflict that Freud identified bears marked similarities to the conflicts every child must live through and often remains embedded in the recesses of the personality, Erikson wishes to focus more explicitly on the 'healthy' personality. He seeks to describe those elements of 'a really healthy personality which are noticeably absent in neurotic patients and which are most obviously present in the kind of man that educational and cultural systems seem to be striving, each in its own way, to create, support and maintain' (Erikson 1968: 52).

However, we may question Erikson's assumption that 'educational and cultural systems' have the right to define a 'really healthy personality'. What criteria are being used to envisage such a paragon, and by whose authority? For example, is such a personality one that subscribes to the 'go for it', 'do it', 'materialistic', 'achieving' philosophy that permeates the US lifestyle? Erikson presents only one definition of the healthy personality. He subscribes to Marie Jahoda's view: 'A healthy personality actively masters his environment, shows a certain unity of personality and is able to perceive the world and himself *correctly*'. Erikson maintains that all the above criteria are relative to a child's cognitive and social development. Again, we may question the exclusive use of the masculine form 'he masters himself', and then wonder at the use of the word '*correctly*', albeit acknowledging that Erikson writes at a time when such language was common.

Erikson postulates that 'once the baby leaves the chemical exchange of the womb for the social exchange system of his society' he is gradually increasing his capacities to meet the opportunities and limitations of his culture. Erikson considers that in his most personal experiences 'the healthy child, given a reasonable amount of guidance and development, can be trusted to obey inner laws of development, laws which create a succession of potentialities for significant interaction with those who teach him' (Erikson 1968: 54).

Erikson writes

> Personality can be said to develop according to steps predetermined in the human organism's readiness to be driven towards, to be aware of, and to interact with widening social radius, beginning with the dim image of a mother and ending with mankind, or at any rate that segment of mankind which counts in the particular individual's life.
>
> (Erikson 1968: 54)

Erikson integrates these developmental ideas into his theory encompassing an overview of the human life cycle, in the eight discrete stages described below.

Erikson's eight-stage life cycle

Stage 1. Infancy: trust versus mistrust
Stage 2. Early childhood: autonomy versus shame and doubt
Stage 3. Play age: initiative versus guilt
Stage 4. School age: industry versus inferiority
Stage 5. Adolescence: identity versus identity diffusion
Stage 6. Early adulthood: intimacy versus self-absorption
Stage 7. Adulthood: generativity versus stagnation
Stage 8. Old age: integrity versus despair

At each stage of life Erikson seeks to describe how baby, child or adult encounters his/her environment. Each stage involves a crisis because 'incipient growth goes together with a shift in instinctual energy, yet causes specific vulnerability' (Erikson 1968: 55).

As the baby grows and develops, radical adjustments such as lying relaxed, sitting securely and running must all be accomplished in their own good time. At the same time the child's interpersonal perspective, too, changes rapidly and often radically, and within a short time span the child can feel conflicting desires. The child may not want to let mother out of sight and yet feel an urge to do things on his/her own and be independent. 'Thus different capacities use different opportunities to become full grown components of the ever new configuration that is the growing personality.' (Erikson 1968: 55)

Erikson thinks that the work of the therapist is to help the patient identify and resolve the paradoxes that occur at each phase. He also accepts a need to work on the often-unresolved residual conflicts from earlier stages. (We may question whether this means such a therapist is likely to enter the relationship with a set of preconceived ideas and is therefore tempted to fit the patient into the therapist's own framework.)

Stage 1. Infancy: trust versus mistrust

Erikson considers that *basic trust* is the cornerstone of the healthy personality. 'The firm establishment of enduring patterns for the solution of the nuclear conflict of basic trust versus mistrust . . . is the first task of the ego.' (Erikson 1965: 241)

Trust is built up through the quality of the relationship with the provider. It is 'a state of being and responding to the sameness and continuity of the outer providers' but also a faith 'in oneself and the capacity of one's own organs to cope with urges' (Erikson 1965: 239). The need for taking in food through the mouth is overwhelming in early babyhood, but the visual and tactile senses are also important. Erikson refers to this stage as the incorporative stage; the baby is receptive to what is being offered.

After 6 months the baby has to learn to seek the nipple without biting and to get used to a form of mutual *regulation*. At this stage there may be a sense of loss as complete unity with the mother is gradually destroyed. 'When/if the baby has the impression of being deprived; divided or abandoned, a residue of mistrust can form.' (Erikson 1968: 63)

However, Erikson highlights that the cultural aspects may be as significant as the instinctual ones. Some cultures swaddle the baby; others leave limbs free. What is good for children and what may happen to them depends on what they are supposed to become and where. For example, American Indians scorned the way the white race allowed babies to cry in the belief that this would make their lungs stronger. But they were proud when their infants became blue in the face with fury when thumped for biting the mother's nipple, believing that the response would make good hunters of them. Therefore even in the earliest encounters human infants meet with all the basic aspects of their culture.

Although the establishment of trust is the first task of maternal care, Erikson concludes that in the current times of change mothers have often lost their own sense of trust in themselves. It is not surprising that Dr Spock began his famous bestseller book for parents with the admonishing first chapter title 'Trust Yourself'.

Stage 2. Early childhood: autonomy versus shame and doubt (2 to 4 years)

Freud called this stage the anal stage, but Erikson sees it as a time when there is emphasis on general muscular achievement and not just on sphincter control. At this stage the infant battles for autonomy and 'the growing ability to hold on and let go, with discretion, to stand "on his own feet" ' (Erikson 1965: 244) (Welchman 2000: 53).

Shame and doubt, the negative consequences of seeking autonomy, are associated with 'being completely exposed and conscious of being looked at' (Erikson 1965: 244). Doubt is linked particularly with having 'a back, an area behind which one cannot see but which may be the source of evil and decay – it is the source of fear of attack from behind' (Welchman 2000: 53).

Erikson's recognition of the link between generations is an interesting feature of his model. At this stage Erikson thinks the adult needs to be firm but tolerant, but that the dignity and autonomy of the child are often dependent on the parents' dignity within the social hierarchy. He considers that much of the 'shame and doubt, the indignity and uncertainty which is aroused in children are a consequence of the parents' frustrations in marriage, work and citizenship' (Erikson 1968: 73).

Stages 3 and 4. Play age: initiative versus guilt (4 to 5 years); School age: industry versus inferiority (5 to 12 years)

By this stage the child has often identified herself as a little person, but must find out what kind of person she wants to be. This is when parents, 'powerful and beautiful' (Erikson 1968: 78), become the role model. Erikson extends Freud's term for this age – 'genital' to 'locomotor genital' – and thus places greater emphasis on the walking and motor activities of this age than did Freud.

Concurrent with the development of movement, language and imagination, the child develops a sense of unbroken initiative. The child often becomes intrusive, invading others' space, sometimes by physical attack, and acquiring knowledge with a consuming curiosity.

The child can perform 'Acts of aggressive manipulation and coercion' (Erikson 1965: 247). This evokes a reaction from significant others and can make the child aware of the hazards in the environment. A sense of badness and fear of punishment evolves, and thus a sense of guilt is born.

There is an infantile sexual curiosity, and Erikson subscribes to the Freudian Oedipal theory that boys develop rivalry with fathers for mother's love and that girls fall in love with their fathers and are jealous of their mothers. Jealous rivalry for the attention of one of the parents and the inevitable failure of this leads to guilt as well as fear and anxiety.

Erikson also accepts Freud's view that girls feel inadequate through penis envy, but thinks that boys can also feel inadequate because the mother dominates the household. Erikson seems to think that the role differentiation prevalent in society is helpful in dispelling early misgivings about sexual difference, although we may wonder if in fact it only serves to reinforce them.

Conscience too begins to develop. This conscience can cause inhibition, regression and resentment if parents do not live up to the standards that they advocate. The child can become convinced that s/he is innately bad, which can lead to self-restriction or a constant need to prove himself by ceaseless 'doing' activity. It is extremely important that carers nurture a sense of worth and responsibility by enterprises such as making things together with the child and other children. Children need to feel equal in worth though different in kind, function or age, to permit a 'peaceful cultivation of initiative'.

Client Ingrid (aged 32), a teacher with a husband and young child, appeared happy and successful yet still felt a deep inner sense of worthlessness and pain. She had suffered from a cruel and emotionally abusive childhood, was never shown any love or respect, and was often subject to her mother's physical violence (and her father's collusion with this). In her late teens and adolescence she had suffered bouts of depression, and she self-harmed to prove that she existed – 'she was not nothing'. She wished to live through these early experiences again in the hope that by so doing she could stop blaming herself and free herself from negative patterns of thought. Through therapy and discussion of her own written accounts of some of these early traumatic experiences, she gained a sense of confidence and for the first time believed that she was 'alright, a person of some worth with something to offer, someone who was capable of living life to the full'.

This is the stage in which children develop 'a sense of industry' and learn to 'win recognition by producing things'. They often feel 'I am what I learn'. Children want to be shown how to get busy with something and how to get busy alongside others. Whereas Freud found this period, when sexuality was only 'latent', relatively uninteresting, Erikson thought that the learning that took place during this time had great significance for the child's future.

School as encouragement to industry

Children in Western society go to school to learn literacy, whereas in less sophisticated societies they learn how to use tools and utensils from adults. In our societies schools seem to be a world of their own, guided by particular goals and limitations (for example, the current standard assessment tests in primary schools), and having little link to the adult world.

Trends in educational philosophy have varied between making schools 'an extension of grim adulthood emphasizing self-restraint and a strict sense of duty' (Erikson 1968: 81) and a place where children can learn by doing what they like to do. Erikson thinks that different children can thrive in both these approaches and that schools need to steer a middle course between work and play.

Play can help a child 'restore a sense of mastery and introduce a child to a world shared with others' (Erikson 1968: 81). It helps a child 'master experience by meditating, experimenting, planning and sharing'.

There is a danger at this stage of the development of a sense of inferiority, particularly if the previous conflicts of the earlier stages have not been resolved. Children may still want the mother or they may not be acknowledged by the teacher for what they have learned to do well earlier at home. The calibre of teachers and the degree to which they understand the child's behaviour are vitally important factors in a child's development. A good teacher can lead a child to positive identification with those who know things and how to do things. A danger is that the child can overidentify, becoming 'teacher's pet'. For many reasons, school can become a totally negative experience and the child never finds there the joy of doing something well.

Here Erikson integrates his social and cultural awareness into his model, by pointing out that this is the period when a child may become aware that their parents' class or race may decide their social worth. He suggests that as a result, it is at this age that lasting harm can be done to the child's sense of identity.

Stage 5. Adolescence: identity versus identity diffusion (12–18 years)

The need for ego identity

Erikson affirms that in human existence there is no feeling of being alive without a sense of ego identity. This term 'identity' is the one most associated with Erikson's work.

Adolescence is the period when the young person often attempts to form a lasting ego identity which is 'the accrued experience of the ego's ability to integrate all identifications with the vicissitudes of the libido, with the aptitudes developed out of endowment, and with the opportunities offered in social roles' (Erikson 1965: 253). All the continuity and certainty of childhood is called into question. In addition, the changes caused by physical and genital maturity in adolescence often coincide with the adolescent's need for consolidation of social roles. Adolescents can become obsessively concerned about how they appear to their peers, wanting to present the 'right' image but feeling that inside they are really someone different from their outer façade. They wonder how to integrate earlier roles into their new sense of identity, and if they are in therapy they may have to return to work on earlier unresolved conflict. They need to develop a sense of ego identity such that they do not feel a discrepancy between their own sense of who they are and their concept of how they appear to others.

This sense of identity can be validated by genuine recognition from significant adults rather than empty praise and condescending encouragement. The adolescent needs to recognize that 'his individual way of mastering experience is a successful variant of the way others around him master such experience'.

Ego identity develops from a gradual integration of all earlier identifications, but the whole has a different quality to the sum of its parts. Erikson asserts that a lasting ego identity cannot exist without the trust of the first oral stage and that the establishment of a confident sense of identity rests on the ongoing promise of fulfilment from significant adult figures in the person's life.

The dangers of identity diffusion

Erikson recognizes that a watering down of the emergent sense of identity, by what he calls 'identity diffusion', causes many of the problems experienced by adolescents. This can happen when the adolescent is assailed by doubts about her ethnic, sexual, religious or class identity.

It is fascinating to study how this ego identity develops and becomes warped in minority groups in America, and I have also observed it in present-day multicultural Britain. The children of immigrants may have a more sensual early childhood, but when their parents begin to mistrust their own traditions in a desperate urge to belong to their adopted culture, they may turn to harsh correctives that cause violent discontinuities. The children themselves then attempt to disown their backgrounds, particularly warm and sensual mothers, as a hindrance to forming a more American or British identity. (See Chapter seven on the development of racial identity.)

The adolescent's sense of identity can be further shaken by exposure to the intolerance of difference and standardization of life-style they experience from their peers in secondary school. Many young people become bewildered by the roles enforced on them by their families and society, and this can result in their dropping out of schools, staying out all night, exhibiting bizarre behaviour or turning to drugs or petty crime. They often gain the label 'delinquent', then live up to the label in a form of self-fulfilling prophecy.

Erikson stresses the importance of occupation at this stage. In the common situation where young people cannot either find or settle in an occupational identity (or indeed a job of any kind) they often turn to the gang, clique or clan. This can lead to a complete merging of themselves, and as a result they may become remarkably intolerant or cruel to all others who are 'different'. Erikson thinks it is important that adults understand such intolerance as a defence against the sense of identity confusion that attacks adolescents in the form of new body images, sexual drives, blossoming relationships and a myriad of conflicting possibilities and choices. This defensiveness is one explanation for the way some young people have found satisfactory identities in simple totalitarian doctrines of race, class and nation. Nazism and the National Front are just two examples. Erikson states

> it is difficult to be tolerant if deep down you are not quite sure whether you are a man or woman, whether you will ever grow together and be attractive, if you will be able to master your drives, that you know who you are, that you know what you want to be, that you know what you look like to others, or whether you will make the right decisions, without committing yourself to the wrong friend, sexual partner, leader or career.
>
> (Erikson 1968: 81)

A gradually emerging ego identity is the adolescent's only safeguard against the anarchy of his drives as well as the autocracy of his conscience, which is usually the inner residue of his past powerlessness in relation to his parents.

> *Client Ingrid developed this identity at a later stage of her life when she realized that her parents' earlier treatment of her was cruel and reprehensible, that she was not responsible for it and that she could reject their values confidently without feeling guilty and diminished.*

Erikson contextualizes his theory within the values of American society. The values that guide identity are linked to his questionable conviction that the 'best people rule and that rule develops the best in people. Young people need to convince themselves that those who succeed are obliged to be the best; by personifying the nation's ideals.' He talks of the special danger that ensues from the presentation of a *synthetic* personality: young people may be deluded into thinking that you are what you can appear to be, or you are what you can buy. This can 'only be counteracted by a system of education which transmits values and goals which determinedly aspire beyond mere functioning and making the grade' (Erikson 1968: 130).

Stage 6: Early adulthood: intimacy versus self-absorption

Erikson was one of the first theorists to identify and focus on life stages in adulthood, and thus gave a lead to later writers such as David Levinson and Naomi Golan. He asserts that it is only after a young person has established a real sense of identity that true intimacy with another can occur. Intimacy is 'the capacity to commit. . . . To concrete affiliations and partnerships and to develop ethical strength to abide by such commitments even though they may call for significant sacrifices or compromises' (Erikson 1965). Relationships and marriage can often be the abortive attempt to find the self through finding another.

The alternative to intimacy is *distantiation*, the readiness to destroy those people and forces that seem to threaten one's own identity. This kind of behaviour can be an extension of reactive adolescent intolerance of difference; it often surfaces and is exploited in politics and war. Sometimes intimate, competitive and combative relations can be experienced with and against the self-same people.

Erikson acknowledges that psychoanalysis emphasizes genitality, the potential to develop orgiastic potency in relation to a loved partner of the opposite sex, as one of the chief signs of the healthy personality. It is also interesting to observe how psychoanalysis stresses that this ideal genitality must be between partners of the *opposite* sex. These views reflect the homophobia endemic in society.

> *They explain the struggles of Daniel, a young gay client who had to leave Ireland and a beloved family at the age of 18 so that he could be true to his gay sexuality. Ten years later he has still been unable to 'come out' to his mother and father.*

> *The concept of working with the polarities between intimacy and distantiation has, however, been useful in therapeutic work with Shane, a 23-year-old student who entered into a regular counselling relationship with a therapist at a youth project. He came with the need to deal with the issue of his dying mother, to whom he was very close. However, the counselling also brought into his awareness his need to separate himself from many domineering members of his family and to develop his own identity after a great deal of invisibility as a young boy. His mother died, and he came to terms with the loss, emerging also with some new insights into his developing self and an intention to relate differently to some of the people close to him.*

Stage 7. Adulthood: generativity versus stagnation

Erikson thinks that sexual mates who have a fulfilled sexual relationship 'will soon wish to combine their personalities and energies in the production and care of offspring'; he calls this *generativity*. He considers this stage a crucial one because it is the link between generations. Again, his focus on the heterosexual couple excludes alternative lifestyles.

However, he does recognize that there are people who are physically unable or who are unwilling to apply this drive to offspring and who divert this wish for responsibility into other channels such as creativity or altruistic concern.

If people do not engage with this stage 'they can experience an obsessive need for pseudo-intimacy with a pervading sense of *stagnation* and interpersonal impoverishment' (Erikson 1968: 258). Such stagnation is important because it affects successive generations. Erikson has found that the majority of parents he sees in child guidance suffer from an inability to develop at this period. He blames negative experiences in early childhood, faulty identification with the parents, excessive self-love and 'lack of father or belief in the species' (Erikson 1968: 258) where there have been no supportive roots in the community.

Stage 8. Old age: integrity versus despair

Erikson is one of the few theorists of personality development who saw old age as a separate life stage with its own tasks and crises and who lived to experience it and reflect upon it personally (he lived to the age of 92). After describing it as the last of the stages in the life cycle (1965), he also he revisits it in *The Life Cycle Completed* (1985), reviewing the stages backwards from old age to infancy. He wishes to see 'How much sense a review of the completed life cycle makes of the whole course' (Erikson 1985: 9). While doing this he emphasizes the final stage as a discrete entity 'and acutely demands new attention and concern in our day' (61) (Welchman 2000: 170). In an age when the proportion of those in Western civilization who survive into their 70s, 80s and 90s is rapidly rising, society can learn much from his observations.

Integrity in the later stages of life is the culmination of the seven stages. It can be achieved 'only in him who in some way has taken care of people and things and has adapted himself to the triumphs and disappointments adherent to being the originator of others or the generator of products and ideas' (Erikson 1968: 259). Erikson claims that people who have achieved this state accept their life cycles and those of significant others. They no longer wish that their parents were different and they accept that they are responsible for their own lives.

Much of the work I did with client Julie hinged on her coming to terms with a distant and insensitive mother and a cold father, releasing her anger and getting on with her life as her own person.

People at this stage have a sense of connection with other human beings who have come before them and who have created 'order, objects and sayings conveying human dignity and love' (1968: 260).

Erikson adds that clinically he has found that despair and a fear of death signify the lack or loss of this ego integration. This despair can take the form of disgust, misanthropy and contempt for institutions and people, and it reflects the individual's own contempt for themself.

Ego integration implies emotional integration, which includes dependency as well as leadership. It involves an awareness of 'the relativity of all the various life styles' but also a readiness 'to defend the dignity of his own life style against all physical and economic threats' (1968: 260). It applies to all aspects of living and all fields of human activity.

In 1989, Erikson, his wife (both in their 80s) and Helen Kivnick, a 30-year-old, wrote '*Vital Involvement in Old Age*'. It centred on interviews with octogenarians who had taken part in the Guidance Study begun in California in 1928. It was an opportunity for Erikson to show how each stage builds on and anticipates the others.

The interviewers tried to understand what enabled elderly people to go on feeling a vital involvement in their own lives and what factors made such an involvement painful, difficult or impossible. 'All these people are struggling to bring lifelong dystonic tendencies into balance with acknowledged strengths.' (1989: 72) As each participant faces the inevitable prospect of death, there is a tension between the integrity they have developed through each stage of life and the despair that this integrity can never be complete, that some opportunities may have been lost for ever and some aspects of their lives wasted.

Erikson concludes that each elderly person tries to balance 'a sense of lifelong wisdom and perspective ... with legitimate feelings of cynicism and hopelessness ...'. Thus each elderly person may achieve an 'ultimate integration' (1989: 72). The interviewers also explore how memory is not just something to be recalled but is adjusted to the needs of the present. One theme, which still recurs in the final stage of life, is the earlier struggle between trust and mistrust. Some old people have no doubt that they would be taken care of despite evidence to the contrary, while others, who had been blaming and mistrustful of people all their lives, were full of ill-founded fear, frequently recalling past affronts and injustices.

The application of the theory to therapy

Erikson's developmental theory can be a useful framework for helping to make sense of a client's world.

Katherine, the wife of an ex-offender came to therapy to try to become more assertive with her unreasonable and bullying husband. She had a real problem in trusting the therapist and it was useful to be able to trace this back to early childhood when her mother had died young and her father had handed her over to a distant aunt. She had learned then that adults could not be trusted to provide safety for her.

However, though the theory may enable insight, we think it is wise to constantly question its relevance and discard what does not seem applicable in the light of present as well as past realities. Katherine's lack of trust could be as easily ascribed to her negative experiences with probation officers and social services, a group of people she perceived as aligned with her therapist.

Daniel Levinson: the seasons of a man's life

In the early 1960s Daniel Levinson, a psychologist, began a research study that was based on his perspective on human life as a series of developmental stages. He specifically focused on a period of human life that had been sadly neglected, mid- and late adulthood. He was aware that a great deal of work had been done on the developmental stages of infancy, childhood and adolescence but little on the middle life period. He researched the period between ages 20 and 45, with particular emphasis on early and mid-life *transitions*.

He considered that the reason for the dearth of reflection and writing on middle age is people's fear in middle age of what the future holds, a fear mainly coloured by the negative view that society holds of old age. Many middle-aged people fear that the next period may be unhappy, unhealthy, dominated by loss of physical capacities and the status often gained through work. It may also be a period permeated by bereavement, with the loss of significant family and friends. For such people, avoidance of reflection is the safest strategy.

Levinson has a more optimistic outlook on the latter 'eras' of life. He sees the life cycle as journey made up of a number of 'seasons' and with an underlying universal pattern and order. The life cycle is an evolving one, which alternates between stable and constructive periods and fluid, changing ones. He considered that if people have knowledge and acceptance of each season of life and the developmental tasks involved, then the later eras can be as fulfilling as any other. Another major reason for his study was his introspective fascination with this era of his own life – he was 46 when he began the project.

By the end of the research, Levinson and his team concluded that there was a pattern and order to the eras of a man's life and that they occur in a fixed sequence. If people are unable to complete the tasks of one era, they become stuck, go into decline and are unable to reach the next developmental period satisfactorily.

> *Client Nita, aged 26, suffered from anorexia and depression. She was unable to free herself from feelings of low self-esteem inflicted by her mother, who wanted her to be a pretty, feminine little girl, always perfectly neat and tidy, when she was not. She needed to achieve the task of separation from her mother and to learn to recognize her own high abilities without being affected by past introjected negative messages. Some of the work of therapy was successfully spent on the achievement of this task.*

Levinson differs from others who considered developmental stages (Kohlberg, Piaget, Loevinger) by giving each era equal significance. He, like Erikson, did not rank them in a hierarchy.

The significance of transitions

Despite stressing the distinction between eras and developmental periods, Levinson also acknowledges the overlaps and that there is considerable interpenetration of one period by another. In some senses, the life cycle is an organic whole and each period contains elements of all the others. He uses Proust to illustrate this point:

> For man is a creature without any fixed age, who has the faculty of becoming, in a few seconds, many years younger, and who surrounded by walls of time through which he has lived, floats with them but as though in a basin, the surface level of which is constantly changing so as to bring him into the range now of one epoch, now of another.
>
> *Remembrance of Things Past*

Consequently Levinson thought that the tasks of the current period could also be the unresolved tasks of previous periods.

> *Fifty-year-old client Una has not freed herself of a childlike dependence on her husband, although she is independent, capable and responsible in many other areas of her life. Part of her therapy involves examining this dependence, her ambivalence over retaining it. She is uncertain over whether she wants the disruptions and arguments she would cause by shedding some of her domestic roles and taking on new roles, such*

as training for a new career and writing (an area where she had considerable talent).

Levinson and his researchers stress the fact that their view of the life cycle has a significance that applies to a range of cultures and societies and had been described by sages and philosophers as far back as 2500 years BC. He quotes at least three ancient versions of 'the ages of man' – The Talmud 'The sayings of the fathers', Confucius 500 BC and Solon, a Greek poet and lawmaker of 700 BC. The distinctive ages of man described by these three coincide remarkably both with each other and with Levinson. However, like Levinson, they all refer only to men and this is a weakness in the research.

The research

Levinson and five of his colleagues at the Psychology Department at Yale University began a research project in 1966 which lasted ten years. The researchers used a sample of 40 men. Since Levinson identified work as the most significant indicator of people's life in society, the men were chosen for their membership of four occupational sub-groups, representing a cross-section of work strata. The groups were: hourly-paid unskilled workers in industry, business executives, university biologists and novelists. Levinson tried to find as diverse a group of men as possible according to the following factors: social class, religion, race, educational background, and marital state – but there were very few who were not white and there were no gay men. The interviewer, like a therapist in the early stages of therapy, gave the men the opportunity to tell their own stories, explore, clarify and make connections. Levinson's conclusions about 'the seasons of a man's life' were based on these biographies.

Obviously any research done on such a small sample of people must have its flaws. However, despite the limitations, there is some relevant material here for therapists whose clients are working through the stresses of mid-life, particularly in the transitional stages.

The eras

Levinson chose to call the different periods of a man's life *eras*, as the word 'era' implies a framework that is broader and more inclusive than the more commonly used term 'stage'. The eras last approximately 25 years, and each era has 'its own distinctive and unifying quality to do with the character of living' (Levinson 1978: 18). An era takes into account biological, psychological and social aspects (not focusing specifically on any one of these) and is consequently broader and more inclusive than other developmental stages. Within each era there are developmental 'periods' lasting roughly five or six years.

1. Pre-adulthood: childhood/adolescence (ages 0–22)
2. *Early childhood transition (0–3)*
3. Early adulthood (17–45)
4. *Early adulthood transition (17–22)*
5. Middle adulthood (40–60)
6. *Mid-life transition (40–45)*
7. Late adulthood (60+)
8. *Late adulthood transition (60–65)*

The transitions

Levinson is also interested in the transitions, the periods of three to four years spanning the change from one era to the next. These have often been acknowledged as times of turbulence, insecurity and sometimes of crisis when people have to consolidate and integrate their past learning and also prepare to face the changes and developmental tasks thrown up by the next era.

In 1981, Naomi Golan, a social worker, also recognized the significance of these periods. She wrote a guide for social workers that particularly focused on transitions. Golan had learned from her work with adults in crisis (starting 18 years earlier) that at certain periods linked to developmental transition (often lasting four or five weeks), people are more vulnerable to acute pressures. On investigating transitional situations she found similarities and parallels in the process that led to further investigations.

She found that an understanding of the issues involved in transitions was a helpful framework when helpers were asked to intervene in critical situations. It was a move away from the tradition of seeing clients' present in terms of their early childhood. She thought it would be useful if professionals could learn the links between personality structure and role expectations during times of heightened change. Golan also found that during developmental bridging periods clients were more amenable to help and found it more effective than at other times.

Early and mid-adulthood

Levinson's research is specifically focused on the age span between 20 and 40. He saw this as a time of the greatest biological abundance and the greatest contradiction and stress. This is the period when the men made major life choices, when they struggled to establish a place in society and in their work, and often moved from novice to senior status. He and his team examined this era from three perspectives:

- Changes in biological and psychological functioning
- The sequence of generations
- The evolution of careers and enterprises.

Erikson and Levinson: similarities and differences

In spite of their different backgrounds and different experience of research with very contrasting client groups, Levinson came to a similar view of the life cycle as Erikson. Levinson's view of the self integrates Erikson's concept of the ego: Levinson's eras and developmental periods roughly equate with Erikson's stages of adult development. Both Levinson and Erikson are deeply concerned with the interconnectedness of self and the world.

However, each of Erikson's stages is governed by a crucial issue concerning how the self relates to the world. The issue is described as a paradox, a contradiction between opposites. The central task of each stage is to resolve these contradictions and integrate them into the whole being.

Although Erikson's stages deal with self in relation to the world, his primary focus is within the person. Each stage is defined in terms of an attribute, for example social commitment, which connects the self to the sociocultural world. He, more than any other, has shown the huge but subtle influence of the sociocultural world on ego development. These studies are particularly fascinating when linked with his interest in the biographical material of such famous figures as Luther, Shaw and Ghandi.

Levinson's approach makes use of Erikson's but shifts the focus. His concept of the life structure places more significance on the *boundaries* between self and the world. It places equal weight on self and the world as aspects of the lived life. Levinson also identifies a larger number of developmental periods and traces the developmental process in more detail. However, Levinson emphasizes that his view builds on and adds to Erikson's and is not antithetical to it.

Levinson considers that people need to work on reconciling the polarities between young and old, destruction and creation, masculine and feminine, and attachment and separateness during the mid-adult transition. Then they can work towards a new place in the life cycle. Although psychologists have studied these polarities in the past, Levinson considered that they are not just aspects of the personality but need to be considered from the perspective of the person within society. More needs to be done to foster such development in pre-adulthood and early adulthood.

During that time men accentuate the young and repress the old, give priority to the masculine and repress the feminine. In youth there is more attachment to the external world in a search for involvement. The young often mask their true feelings and feel a strong need to be in control. In mid-adulthood a man can develop a stronger sense of self and separateness from the world.

There is a strong individual and institutional reluctance to look more deeply at new questions that invoke anxiety. Levinson says that the paradox is that 'we must devote ourselves to a search for new solutions even though we are not up to the task and it will take generations more of muddling through before significant advance can be made' (1978: 340). In the longer run, our further progress in fostering adult development must be a part of a transformation of human society and personality and thus contribute to a new epoch in human development. At the start of a new millenium this could be a lodestar.

Client Leila, aged 41, came to therapy because she had courageously decided to change her life. She had given up a well-paid and secure job because it did not meet her inner needs for fulfillment. She was in the process of ending a destructive love relationship. At this crisis point of transition in her life she was able to reflect on her past experiences and how they had shaped her. She began to replace an inner insecurity and need to please others by valuing her personal qualities of warmth, generosity and competence, and she gained a stronger belief in herself. She started to reconcile her inner paradoxes and to move towards new directions in a positive and creative way.

C H A P T E R 3

Personality development in person-centred theory

Val Simanowitz

Leading theorists and practitioners of the person-centred approach, such as Carl Rogers, Brian Thorne, David Mearns and Godfrey Barrett-Lennard, perceive the development of personality throughout the life cycle in a distinctively different way from the more orthodox theorists of the psychoanalytical and behavioural schools.

One of Rogers' most radical ideas was his wish to free himself from the constraints of those theories and base his conclusions on his experience of working with people from within their own subjective frame of reference rather than approaching clients with a set of pre-conceptions. From his experience followed another of Rogers' central beliefs, that, at some deep level, the client knows what is best for themself and if they participate in a particular kind of interpersonal relationship based on a climate of trust they will access this knowledge.

In general, person-centred theorists, therefore, wishing to avoid working from within a prescribed framework, do not perceive the development of personality as a series of discrete stages but as a fluid, flexible and evolving process.

Elements of developmental theory in Rogers' 19 propositions

In 'A Theory of Personality and Behaviour' (Rogers 1951: 481–533) Rogers makes 19 theoretical statements that incorporate his ideas on personality development. However, in these propositions he not only describes the development of personality through childhood but also what causes discord, disturbance, distortion and denial. His theory outlines the conditions he considers most favourable to enable a person to become aware of their true inner self, to recognize such disturbance and to change in order to deal with the discord.

These propositions also include a model of the person Rogers considers we should aspire towards – the integrated, self-fulfilled person. While acknowledging that this is a person we can *aspire towards* rather than become, this model is a clear vision of what people *could* reach, after gaining deep insights into themselves and possibly at the conclusion of successful therapy.

A strong underlying foundation of the approach is Rogers' belief that all biological organisms (plants and animals), and thus all people, in their journey from the cradle to the grave move towards becoming the best they can possibly be (Rogers 1959). This movement is called the *actualizing tendency* and is based on the ideas of earlier humanistic theorists such as Abraham H. Maslow and Rollo May.

This theory resonated too with the context and spirit of early twentieth-century America, a country full of new immigrants, many of them leaving behind the persecution and oppression of hierarchical and cynical Europe: a country where everything was possible and it seemed the only requirement was the energy and drive to 'go for it'. This belief in individual fulfilment is not just a phenomenon of contemporary America. It goes right back to Classical Greek Platonic ideas and to the philosophies of the Renaissance.

All Rogers' theories are deeply imbued with the concept of growth and the importance of the therapist creating a climate conducive to the development of such growth. He distinguishes between the actualization of the *organism* (the whole self of the human being, encompassing the physical, the cognitive, the emotional and the spiritual) and the actualization of the *self* (the person's concept of their own identity).

> It should be noted that this basic actualising tendency is the only motive which is postulated in this theoretical system. It should also be noted that it is the organism as a whole and only the organism as a whole, which exhibits this tendency . . . The self, for example is an important construct in our theory, but the self does not do anything. It is only one expression of the general tendency in the organism to behave in those ways which maintain and enhance the self
>
> (Rogers 1951: 487)

Perhaps it is intrinsic to the nature of counselling work, but in my 25 years as a practitioner, I have never experienced a client without a tendency to move towards actualization in spite of self-destructive and negative behaviours, depression, or periods of stuckness.

> *Client Barbara is a waif-like, lonely and self-abnegating woman in her 50s, whose life had been dominated by her obsessive/compulsive and agoraphobic behaviours for more than 30 years. She is depressed and unhappy, cannot leave the house alone and sleeps little, having to get up frequently in the night to check if she has turned off gas and electricity. Yet she maintains a strong strand that looks forward to the time when she can operate and function in a more 'normal' fashion, and she has made keen efforts to struggle towards this.*

There are, of course, examples of people who cannot escape from self-destructive behaviours, which often means they cannot become clients or benefit from counselling. Sometimes, sadly for these people, dying is the alternative to actualizing.

The development of the self and the self-concept

The self Rogers states that as the infant develops, she begins to recognize a portion of her private world as 'I' 'Me' 'Myself'. The infant experiences those elements they control as part of the self; if less controlled, they become less part of the self.

The self-concept As people develop, a *self-concept* emerges that is often different from the true organismic inner self. The self-concept is the individual's personal construction of himself, which has developed in response to significant others. As parents, carers and teachers praise or blame, show warmth or repress and criticize, the child begins to believe these evaluative messages and to accept them as an integral part of himself.

From close observation of his clients, who could be confident and coping one session and have a sense of utter worthlessness in the next, Rogers came to think that the self is not a fixed entity but the product of the people's response to their experience of their perception of themselves in relation to others. As Brian Thorne puts it,

> I am the self which I currently conceptualize myself as being. This conceptualization, however, is dependent not only on thousands

of experiences and conditionings which constitute my past but also on unpredictable events and interactions which may occur at any moment. It is possible for me to experience my 'self' as happy, confident and assured at one moment and despairing, inadequate and demoralized the next.

(Thorne 1992: 29)

Conditions of worth

Rogers stresses that in person-centred theory the most important aspect of childhood is how much the child experiences love and trust from the parents. From Victorian times onwards, influenced by the morality of punitive religious doctrine, many parents believed that strict discipline towards a child led to good character. They were very parsimonious with praise but extremely critical of characteristics that did not conform to society, were inconvenient to their lifestyle or, in cases of poorer families, interfered with the family's ability to earn a living. As a consequence, many children have grown up with very low self-esteem and negative concepts of themselves, weighed down by guilt and shame. This, of course, resonates with psychoanalytical theory such as Erikson's stages 1 and 2. Rogers has concluded that most children experience 'conditions of worth' and receive love only with strings attached.

As the child's awareness develops there is a new need, the 'need for positive regard' and in Rogers' words this is 'pervasive and persistent' (Rogers 1959: 223). The satisfaction of the need becomes the major concern of the growing child, greater than the need to respond to the actualizing tendency. This need for positive regard is inextricably linked to the child's need to develop self-regard. Without overt positive regard, a child's self-regard is stunted in growth and often a withered and twisted self-concept emerges. If infants are surrounded by critical and repressive people, or those who give confused or conflicting signals, they become confused and are forever seeking 'ways to win at least the occasional sign of love or affection' (Thorne 1992: 30).

Thorne continues by stating that

> our positive regard can become totally dependent on the quality and consistency of the regard shown to us by others and where this has been selective (as to some degree it must be for all of us) we are the victims of *conditions of worth*. We have worth in our

own eyes only on condition that we think, feel and behave in ways that other people have told us are worthy of love and respect. At worst this can result in a situation where 'authentic living is well nigh impossible'.

(Thorne 1992: 31)

There are parallels here with Winnicott's views about the child's development of a false self.

An anorexic (27-year-old) client, Nora, had experienced her mother's withdrawal of love whenever, as a child, she followed her natural desire to dress in scruffy clothes and play boisterous games. She was only approved of when she wore neat, pretty dresses and was 'nice and polite' to her elders. She developed extremely low self-esteem and was constantly trying to live up to her mother's desired image. Conditions of worth had made her lose touch with her physical, playful self. Later, as a teenager, at school she needed to live up to her peers' standards and to the requirement to be slim as dictated by media, adverts and magazines.

Through the non-judgmental and accepting attitude of the therapist she began to value positive aspects of herself (she was extremely clever and competent at office and administrative work). Her use of imagery enabled her to see the anorexia as a negative and parasitical 'octopus' from which she had to struggle to disentangle herself, rather than as an asset to her life. She learned to accept that she could not be completely in control of her world and that she would have to live with some degree of uncertainty. After two years, although the anorexia had not completely disappeared, she was able to hold down a demanding job and form a fulfilling, serious relationship with a new boyfriend.

The locus of evaluation/The outcomes of conditions of worth

The outcome of strong conditions of worth in childhood can be a weak or external 'locus of evaluation'. This locus of evaluation is a person's 'deep inner source of wisdom' (Mearns and Thorne 1988: 10). Rogers maintained that those who strongly desire the approval of significant others and do not gain that approval have lost touch with their inner guiding sense of how to behave, or have an external locus of evaluation. However, when the locus of evaluation is accessible and the person can act on it without fear or too much hesitation, then it is 'internal'. Often one of the aims of person-centred counselling is to enable a person to exchange an external locus of evaluation for an internal one.

Nora learned through therapy what she had deeply sensed but denied before. She began to acknowledge that her adventurous spirit was an asset rather than evidence that she was 'unnatural', and that, for example, she had a right to enjoy her love of motor bikes or any other such 'tomboyish' pursuits.

Disturbance, distortion, denial

Although Rogers has often been criticized for focusing too much on the optimistic and the positive, a significant portion of the 19 propositions is devoted to examining the results of negative childhood experiences such as conditions of worth. Rogers gives the example that if the child has angry feelings and parents are strongly critical, these feelings are denied and inner discord arises. However, if the parents, without threatening to withdraw love, accepts these feelings, the child does not need to deny the feelings or distort the parents' reaction and integrate it as their own. The child can begin to develop a secure self.

As a consequence of too many critical messages, children can take in other people's view of them as a reality (introject). Children can ignore what does not fit with this new, adopted view of reality, or they can pretend it did not happen or distort it to make it fit. These childhood experiences can be the beginning of the maintenance of a false façade in adulthood, which can operate as a successful mask. However, Rogers says that often below the seemingly successful surface people are troubled.

'*Incongruence* between self and experience involves a state of vulnerability and a degree of dysfunction.' When such people experience something inconsistent with this self-concept they become anxious within themselves, they are very likely to be unhappy and have low self-esteem. The cost of the defence they erect in order to be acceptable to themselves can include 'a tightness or rigidity of perception and the potential of intense arousal or over-reactivity, in some areas.' (Rogers 1959: 227). Sometimes it is only a traumatic episode, such as the loss of a parent or partner, which stimulates such individuals to look at themselves and perhaps seek therapy.

David Mearns' and Brian Thorne's developments of Rogers' theory: configurations of self

David Mearns and Brian Thorne have developed this element of Rogers' theory of self to include the idea that when a person has internalized the messages or orders from significant others, an alternative dimension of personality, what they call a *configuration* may develop. 'A configuration is a hypothetical construct denoting a coherent pattern of feelings, thoughts and preferred behavioural responses symbolized or pre-symbolized by the person as reflective of a dimension of existence within the Self.' (Thorne and Mearns 2000) Mearns and Thorne examine Rogers' proposition.

> Behaviour may, in some instances, be brought about by organic experiences and needs which have not been symbolized. Such behaviour may be inconsistent with the structure of the self, but in such instances the behaviour is not 'owned' by the individual.
> (Rogers 1952: 509)

They reflect that he might want to add the following

> In some cases the behaviour may be '*owned*' but allocated to a part, or *configuration* within the self. Such a configuration may well be inconsistent with other parts of the Self and carry restricted access.
> (Mearns and Thorne 2000: 117)

Mearns and Thorne think that such a configuration may become strongly influential in a personality. Once it is established, it will

> voraciously assimilate other consistent elements. It may become '*an organizing principle*' which can lend structure and function to individual thoughts, feelings and self experiences ... For example a configuration carrying the narrative that a person is 'untrustworthy' might readily expand to include the message that they are also 'unlovable' on the basis of minimal evidence.
> (Mearns and Thorne 2000: 118)

Pat is a middle-aged woman with low self-esteem, obsessed with her poor educational background and what she considers her poor perform-ance as a GP's practice manager. She often switches to victim/child configuration, denigrating herself and full of anxiety. (In fact her work

*is of a very high standard and she is a perfectionist.) She had internal-
ized her mother's endless instructions to do better, reach the same level
as her clever sister and never express anger. It was only when her
mother died that she came to therapy. The therapist recognized this
'poor child' configuration and enabled Pat to bring it into awareness. It
fitted Pat's perception of herself and she and her therapist are working
with it and also with Pat, the adult woman.*

Mearns and Thorne acknowledge a resemblance to object relations
theory (Fairbairn 1952) and to Transactional Analysis (Berne 1961).
However, they focus more on configurations as dynamic and evolving rather than static and non-changing. They see the human
being as a

dynamic, interactive event in evolution. The configurations
within the self are not permanently compartmentalized like psychic 'scabs'. Each of these 'parts' needs to serve its protective
function more effectively. This development is facilitated by the
inter-relating of configurations within the Self.

(Mearns and Thorne 2000: 118)

Mearns and Thorne have also developed Rogers' ideas about the
actualizing tendency in their dialogical person-centred theory of self.
They consider that it is extremely important for a therapist and client
to be aware of and to work with whatever issues block the actualizing
tendency and inhibit growth. Mearns was inspired to develop this
work by his experience of clients who 'express caution when faced
with the urge to move or change' (Mearns and Thorne 2000: 177).
Whereas Rogers saw these blocks as hindrances, Mearns sees them as
positives and an asset to effective work. Mearns considers that after
Rogers moved to the west coast and the person-centred approach was
in its 'so called California period', the strong emphasis on the positive
and moving forward led to a 'tyranny of growth' which became
unbalanced.

Mearns sees clients' cautionary elements as

important survival mechanisms, which have been fundamental
to earlier development. They help a person mediate the pace of
growth and keep contact with the social structures of life which if
maintained, can offer considerable orchestration for future
growth.

(2000: 177)

He thinks that psychological health is not a matter of overcoming these restrictive forces but of restoring an appropriate balance between the clients' forms of *social mediation* (complying with the expectations of the society in which they operate) and the actualizing tendency.

> *Miriam, 43, a deputy head teacher and single parent, hated the restrictions, bureaucracy and heavy workload, which stopped her from doing effective work, but considered it necessary to continue in her job for financial reasons and particularly to help support her teenagers in education. Although her inner self yearned for change, the therapist needed to work with the forces that restrained her from resigning. Miriam came to accept that for three or four years that was how her life would be: she tried to cut down her workload as much as possible and to give herself some time for friends and her own interests. She realized that for her own mental health, she had to operate within the system not confront it head-on, like Don Quixote, at every opportunity.*

Conditions conducive to awareness and change

Rogers postulates that the quality of our relationships with others is of paramount importance and is the essence of therapy. If we can develop a relationship of trust with another person and such a person can accept us without conditions, be genuine with us and fully understand our perception of the world, then there is a climate for awareness, reflection and growth. We can examine our picture of ourselves and identify what does not fit. We may change this picture, or we may be better able to live with the discrepancies having once recognized them as a source of anxiety. Rogers considers that once we are more accepting of ourselves as we truly are, we can begin to understand and value both the similarity and diversities of others. We can abandon rigid value systems and adopt values more in line with our own experience rather than live according to the values of others.

> *Hilary, a social worker in her early 50s, has a sense of low self-esteem, an indeterminate locus of evaluation and a deep inner dissatisfaction with the stresses of her life. She feels a clash between her principled approach to working in the interests of clients and the demands made on her to conform to new financially dictated norms of 'managed care'. Her wishes for success and her envy of those who rise to high positions*

clashes with her deeper principles, causing stress and insecurity. Part of the work of counselling is to establish trust to enable her to examine how her self-concept has developed and to recognize and be guided by her own inner sense of wisdom (locus of evaluation). She has begun to be more assertive at meetings and to trust her own perceptions more, but again has to learn not to allow the assertiveness to spill over into an aggression that alienates her managers and is counterproductive to her aims.

The fully functioning person

The concluding propositions in Rogers' personality theory imply that if the process of actualization is allowed to develop unimpeded by conditions of worth, an 'actualized' being might result. In 1959 Rogers tried to elaborate on and describe the characteristics of such an actualized or fully functioning person. As stated earlier, the characteristics of such a person are always part of an evolving process and it is self-evident that people can more realistically work towards these ideals than actually attain them. Merry (1999: 28) sets out what these might be:

A fully functioning person would

- Be open to experience
- Exhibit no defensiveness
- Be able to interpret experience accurately
- Have a flexible rather than a static self-concept, open to change through experience
- Trust in his or her own experiencing process and develop values in accordance with that experience
- Have no conditions of worth and experience unconditional self-regard
- Be able to respond to new experiences openly
- Be guided by his or her own valuing process through being fully aware of all experience, without the need for denial or distortion of any of it
- Be open to feedback from his or her environment and make realistic changes resulting from that feedback
- Live in harmony with others and experience the rewards of mutual positive regard.

Rogers is convinced that there could be personality development, moving a client towards full functioning, through counselling. He envisages that the development that could take place through the therapeutic relationship and the core conditions is similar to the process that could take place in childhood, if it were not warped and marred by the interventions of parents, carers, teachers and others (however well-meaning they might think they are).

Rogers focuses, above all, on process and sees a distinct pattern to it. He sees change in therapy thus

> . . . the essential direction was from a relatively fixed, self perpetuating quality, to an open, flowing, self transcending quality: from fixity and recycling motion to a formative changingness; briefly from a condition of stasis to one of process.
>
> (Barrett-Lennard 1998: 83)

The seven-stage developmental model of counselling

Rogers' seven-stage model of counselling reflects how the healthy personality might have developed untrammelled by the inevitable constraints of the society around it. This model explains how the counsellor and client can work to counteract negative patterns. Merry summarizes these stages in *Learning and Being in Person-centred Counselling* (1999: 50).

Stage 1

People at Stage 1 are very rigid, out of touch with their feelings, judgemental and pessimistic. They blame others and consider revelation of feelings to be a weakness. It is unlikely that such people would be in counselling, but we have all encountered clients who have been 'sent' to counselling by concerned family, partners, teachers, probation officers or even courts of law.

Stage 2

The rigidity is loosening but people are unlikely to accept responsibility for themselves. They feel like victims. Again, they blame the world for whatever is wrong.

Stage 3

These people are more willing to talk about themselves, although they may use the impersonal distancing language of 'you', 'one' or 'we'. They are more comfortable talking about feelings of the past rather than the present. They may become aware of internal contradictions. They perceive the world in terms of clear opposites.

Roger, an ex-alcoholic who had had a bleak, poverty-stricken and loveless childhood, strongly redolent of Frank McCourt's in Angela's Ashes, *arrived for counselling in this stage. However, once he had identified some of the contradictions in himself and had taken responsibility for his own strictness in dealing with his adolescent children (despite the adverse effects this kind of treatment had had on him), he became more ready to acknowledge his feelings and move towards the next stage.*

Stage 4

People can talk more about their feelings, although they have difficulty in understanding and accepting the negative. People become more aware of the 'here and now' relationship with the counsellor and can observe it openly.

Roger became aware that he had never talked about his feelings on the birth of a daughter with spina bifida and that it felt cathartic to be able to do so. He acknowledged that it was only after he had learned to trust the therapist (after an initial three-month period of mistrust) that he felt free to do this.

Stage 5

People begin to feel confident about expressing presently experienced feelings. They can get near to something important but still avoid direct contact with it. New insights may begin to emerge.

Roger was able to express his rage at the reaction of one of his friends to the birth of his daughter with a disability. (The friend had suggested that it would have been kinder to 'put her down'.)

Stage 6

At this stage the client can begin to express previously suppressed feelings in the moment. The self is less fragmented and more whole. The client begins to view the world in a new way. Internal communication is free and relatively unblocked.

> *Roger was more able to admit his shortcomings, such as his tendency to explode at his adolescent children: he was more willing to work on improving his relationships with them.*

Stage 7

By this stage people are making changes for themselves in their own lives and translating their learning into realities.

> *Roger got a steady and well-paid job, improved his relationships with his family by engaging in open dialogue with them and started some counsellor training himself, believing his past experiences and new insights would enable him to offer something to others.*

Rogers stresses that the seven stages vary from client to client and counsellor to counsellor – they are not a prescription for the course counselling should take.

M. Cooper on person-centred developmental theory

Some more recent person-centred theorists (M. Cooper, 'Developing the person-centred theory of development' 2000) contend that person-centred practitioners cannot stand completely outside a developmental framework.

> The choice therefore is not whether person-centred practitioners do or don't have developmental assumptions. Rather the choice is whether the person-centred practitioners allow their develop-mental assumptions to stagnate and influence their practice in unreflective ways. Or whether person-centred practitioners keep their developmental assumptions fluid and alive, and thereby

ensure that they continue to engage their clients in fluid, open
and self reflective ways.

(2000: 1)

Cooper in his article is attempting to keep his developmental assumptions fluid and alive by re-examining some of Rogers' developmental
concepts. He particularly focuses on the actualizing tendency and what
conflicts are intrinsic to it, thus preventing it from moving forward.

Many commentators have concluded that there is a split between
the actualizing tendency and self-actualizing, perhaps similar to the
split between the organismic self and the self-concept. Cooper thinks
that Rogers was not perceiving this as a basic split, because a part
cannot be split completely if it is integral to a whole.

> A more consistent way of understanding Rogers' fundamental
> development conflict then, would be to construe it as a conflict
> between the self-actualizing tendency and non self-actualizing
> subsystems of the actualizing tendency, such as the tendency to
> actualize one's creative potential, or the tendency to actualize
> one's potential; to nurture . . . in other words, Rogers' develop-
> mental model can be understood to propose that the organism
> inhibits a world in which to actualize one potentiality – its self – it
> must inhibit the actualization of other potentialities. The organ-
> ism, therefore, is understood to be a continually actualizing being,
> but a being that becomes divided and skewed because its world will
> only allow it to actualize one potentiality at the expense of another.
>
> (2000: 2–3)

Cooper gives the example of a young working-class father who wishes
to be a dancer but also wishes to provide financial support for his
family. He might have to choose between training as a dancer and
earning little causing his family suffering and doing a mundane
boring job. The issue here is not just his need to maintain the self-
concept and his wish for positive regard, other aspects of the actualizing tendency are in conflict. Cooper maintains that to understand
how the actualizing tendency is thwarted, person-centred theorists
may need to move away from a developmental model that focuses too
exclusively on the development of 'self'.

Cooper says that there are a number of different ways in which a
person develops beliefs about who she is and these are not necessarily linked to a need for positive self-regard. He refers to Cooley (1902)
and the symbolic interactionists, who state that the way we see

ourselves is dependent on how we imagine others see us. He refers to Sartre and the existentialists, who say we construct a concrete idea of who we are to ward off the anxiety of an ungrounded existence. He also refers to Berne (1961) and the transactional analysts, who say we retain concepts of self from earlier periods of life (for example, the free and adapted child). In the light of these and other theories, Cooper sees a need to widen Rogers' theory and suggests that the concept of self may be derived from multiple sources. Consequently there may be multiple self-concepts. (See this chapter p. 57, Mearns and Thorne.)

Cooper concludes that there is a need to broaden out Rogers' 1959 model of human development. The estrangement of the organism from its true self is not the only means of inhibiting the move towards actualization. Cooper argues that there is the possibility of multiple aspects of the actualizing tendency coming into conflict, the development of multiple selves from multiple sources and the denial and distortion of organismic experiences for multiple reasons. Rogers' theory is only one aspect of how people develop in the way that they do. Thus the person-centred practitioner does not have to fit her client into this framework but can consider other aspects of how the actualizing organism comes to turn against itself. Theorists and practitioners can, for example, examine the effects of adverse socio-political conditions (2000: 6).

Rogers was revolutionary in his time, reacting strongly to the rigid assessment, diagnostic, prescriptive and interpretative methods practised by psychologists and analysts and critical of both the medical and behavioural models. However, in his attempts to eschew contemporary developmental and therapeutic theory and focus on the mutual and reciprocal elements of the therapeutic relationship, he may well have been avoiding facing some important issues.

Firstly, as acknowledged by Cooper *et al.*, many therapists will probably be unable to bracket their previous knowledge of developmental theory and will, through their own conditioning and upbringing, implicitly accept certain norms. It may then be wiser to acknowledge, be aware of and reflect thoughtfully on our own developmental frameworks rather than attempt to dismiss them. Secondly, some contemporary person-centred theorists, for example Mearns and Thorne, have identified some gaps in Rogers' hypotheses, and have integrated some developmental variations, such as configurations and the dialogical self, into Rogers' theoretical framework. Thirdly, Rogers' ideal of an equal relationship between therapist and client may be unattainable, and we may need to acknowledge our 'power' in order to use it to empower our clients rather than deny or abuse it.

C H A P T E R **4**

Existential approaches

Peter Pearce

Background

There is no one theorist who can solely be credited with the emergence of the philosophical ideas known as existentialism. These ideas may, therefore, be thought of as a set of attitudes or an approach to life, rather than as one coherent body of theory. The ideas of the Danish philosopher Søren Kierkegaard and the German philosopher Friedrich Nietzsche, both writing towards the end of the nineteenth century, though very different from one another, provided the underpinnings. Philosophically these ideas were continued in the twentieth century by the work of Martin Heidegger, Jean-Paul Sartre and others. Similarly, there have been a number of therapists from different schools of thought who have sought to integrate this philosophy into an approach to therapy. Amongst them, in Europe, Ludwig Binswanger, Victor Frankl and Medard Boss, and translating these ideas into the climate of post-World War II America, Rollo May and later Irvin Yalom.

Existential psychology arose as a response to the prevailing psychodynamic and behavioural schools of thought, both of which were seen to take a somewhat reductionist and deterministic approach to humanity. In other words, both of them reduced the human experience to its component parts and suggested in different ways that we are determined by our past. This clearly influences the approach of the existential psychotherapist towards human development, with a quite distinct approach from the more traditional psychodynamic or cognitive models, which in the main concentrate upon age-appropriate stages.

Scientific reductionism versus (inter) subjectivity

Existentialists believe that something is lost in the attempt to analyse component parts, and thus believe that a so-called 'objective' scientific method is a flawed way to make sense of the human condition. Instead, they do not attempt to separate subject and object, or what is experienced from what is experiencing (intentionality). Instead they take as their starting point the *lived experience* of the person. Kierkegaard argued that truth cannot be seen as something separate from human experience, it can only be uncovered by beginning with the person's perception of it. So truth for existentialists is relational and the starting point for study is thus moment to moment, subjective experience, using what is known as the *phenomenological approach*: that is, paying attention to the immediacy of felt sensation to make sense of experience (phenomenon) without interpretation. Phenomenology requires that we 'bracket', or put to one side, the idea of what something really is, the objective reality of it.

Scientific determinism versus freedom and choice

Existentialists emphasize freedom and choice, though they do not deny that there are real limitations. For the existentialist, however restrictive the external environment may be, we are always more than the victim of circumstances. We are not purely determined by our past, by biology or by society; rather we create ourselves through our choices. May (1953) describes how 'consciousness of self gives us the power to stand outside the rigid chain of stimulus and response, to pause, and by this pause to throw some weight on either side, to cast some decision about what the response will be'.

Thus we always have some freedom. Sartre points out that life is a continuous process of choice-making and that there is no escape from this, saying, 'we are condemned to choose'. The goal for existentialists is to accept the personal responsibility for this freedom of choice and in doing so, move from determinism to 'destiny' (May, 1967). For Sartre, 'we are our choices', and to fail to accept responsibility for our choices is therefore to be 'inauthentic' or to be in 'bad faith' (1956). There is movement, therefore, but not from stage to stage, but between different forms of consciousness.

'Thrownness'

Existentialists acknowledge how, as humans, we are 'thrown' into the world, having no control over the timing and context of our birth. We therefore begin making choices from this position of having already had much decided for us. We come into a pre-existing sociopolitical and cultural context, inheriting our genetics and family setting.

Existentialists emphasize uncovering and accepting the givens in life and the personal limitations for any of us. Sartre (1956) calls this 'facticity' and Binswanger (1958) the 'ground' or 'thrownness' of existence. By paying attention to these givens we become authentically aware of what we are able to influence. Frankl vividly described how an awareness of the severe limitations imposed on his and others' freedoms as a prisoner in a concentration camp enabled recognition of what freedoms remained and contributed to the ability to survive. The opposite of this, believing we have no choice when we do, can be very restricting. Maddi (1996: 163) describes how, 'the confusion of possibilities as necessities lies at the heart of psychopathology, according to existentialists.' People in this situation lack the courage necessary to take responsibility for themselves and live authentically.

Authenticity

To achieve authentic existence is seen as the defining character of humanity and involves thinking and awareness. To act authentically is to decide for ourselves on the personal meaning we derive from life and to act in accordance with this meaning – to be who we are. Existentialism emphasizes that there is no intrinsic meaning in life. We must accept meaninglessness and fully engage with the lifelong task of becoming, of creating our own unique meaning. Frankl (quoting Nietzsche) describes how, 'he who has a why to live can bear with almost any how'. Sartre (1956) refers to human existence as nothingness, literally no-thing-ness, emphasizing this lack of intrinsic essence. He eloquently describes the active task of creating ourselves, 'our existences precede our essences'.

Ontological anxiety

So life involves a constant process of decision-making whatever the 'givens' of our circumstances, and taking the responsibility of this freedom of choice is demanding. It leads to what existentialists call ontological anxiety, or the 'anxiety of being'. This anxiety is an inevitable part of being human, though people often attempt to avoid it through a refusal to exercise the freedom to be. In the short term abnegating this responsibility and conforming to the expectations of others may provide some relief from ontological anxiety. However, such inauthentic living is accompanied by ontological guilt or regret about missed opportunity. For existentialists we are often faced with a stark choice between a known (familiar) and an unknown. Making a choice for the unknown moves us into the future but brings with it unavoidable ontological anxiety. Making the conforming choice of the known is choosing the past and brings up ontological guilt. Ideal and authentic living is seen in having the 'courage' (May 1953: 191) to choose the future and accept the inevitable accompanying anxiety.

A number of different sources of ontological anxiety have been identified, centring around death, freedom of choice, isolation and meaninglessness. Yalom (1980) describes these as the four 'ultimate concerns'.

- *Death*: knowledge of the finiteness of life and the inevitability of death brings anxiety. An authentic response to this is to attempt to live as fully as is possible. May (1981) describes how awareness of death can be a source of creativity and zest for life. In facing the inevitability of death, we have the possibility of coming to an understanding of life.
- *Freedom*: the necessity to continuously chose our future when so much is unknown and uncertain raises a fear of failure. An authentic response to this is to take responsibility for our choices and our lives. Life is predetermined when we are unaware of our choices. When we become aware of how we already are making choices we can move from determinism to destiny.
- *Isolation*: the knowledge that we enter life alone and can never be fully understood by, or understand, others gives rise to anxiety about isolation. An authentic response is to accept the reality of ultimate aloneness, try to become known to ourselves and attempt to reach out to others, to know them and to become known by them.
- *Meaninglessness*: the lack of inherent meaning in life gives rise to anxiety. An authentic response is to attempt to create a personal meaning for life. Frankl (1985: 166) describes this felt meaninglessness as the 'existential vacuum', an emptiness that people neurotically try to fill. Depression, addiction and aggression may result, described by Frankl as the 'mass neurotic triad'.

- *Conformity and neurotic anxiety*: many people seek meaning outside of themselves in conformity or do not take responsibility for their choice-making, becoming what others expect them to be. Ultimately this leads to them feeling alienated from themselves. Tillich (1952) acknowledges the courage that it takes to learn how to live from the inside.

Having the courage to face such ontological anxiety is demanding and, of course, everyone has some accumulated ontological guilt from missed opportunities. Importantly, this too must be accepted; attempting to deny it leads to being inauthentic.

Anxiety cannot be permanently avoided through denial and conformity. Attempting to escape anxiety in these ways is likely to lead to what May (1967) describes as 'neurotic anxiety' and guilt. Normal anxiety is a natural, inescapable aspect of life and growth, to be accepted and endured. Neurotic anxiety is a consequence of the inability to face the normal anxiety as it arises. Anxiety becomes out of proportion to the trigger, becoming associated with a person's entire being.

Being-in-the-world

For existentialists, 'being', what Binswanger (1963) describes as 'being-in-the-world', is an active process of decision-making and therefore, unlike Rogers' (1959: 244) 'actualizing tendency', is a quality only experienced by humans, not by all life. The concept of being-in-the-world tries to capture the idea that person and environment are part of a continuous whole. They cannot be made sense of separately. It is also intended to evoke the subjective experience of both, being and world.

Three modes of being-in-the-world have been differentiated: Umwelt, or 'world around'; Mitwelt, or 'with world'; and Eigenwelt, or 'own world' (May 1958; Frankl 1959; Binswanger 1963). These terms are not intended to refer to some shared objective reality but rather to describe subjective experience. So Umwelt describes a person's relationship to the natural world of biological needs, drives and instincts; Mitwelt, a person's relationship to their social, interpersonal interactions; and Eigenwelt, a person's self-awareness and relationship to themself. May (1983) emphasizes that human beings simultaneously exist in each of these worlds and therefore any understanding of the individual needs to consider each of these modes.

Existential views on personality development

Because of their emphasis upon subjectivity and phenomenological enquiry, many existential theorists have not felt it appropriate to delineate theories of development. There has been a broad emphasis upon authentic as opposed to inauthentic modes of being. May (1953), though not producing a detailed developmental theory, has discussed the development process as centring around the themes of dependency and autonomy. The infant is physically and psychologically dependent at birth. Physical dependency decreases as the child develops. Movement towards maturation depends upon how issues of psychological dependency are met.

May (1953) describes how 'the conflict is between every human being's need to struggle towards enlarged self-awareness, maturity, freedom and responsibility and his tendency to remain a child and cling to the protection of parents or parental substitutes'. Healthy development requires individuals to have the courage to assume responsibility for themselves rather than allow themselves to be defined by others. He outlines four stages of consciousness in the development process: innocence, rebellion, ordinary consciousness of self and creative consciousness of self.

- *Innocence*: this describes the infant, having little or no experience of consciousness.
- *Rebellion*: this defiant, reactive, oppositional consciousness is the first expression of inner strength. The terrible twos and adolescent/teen rebellion describe the action of this stage.
- *Ordinary consciousness of self*: this stage is reached when the individual is capable of learning from mistakes and taking responsibility for their actions.
- *Creative consciousness of self*: akin to Maslow's 'peak experiences', this describes moments when ordinary consciousness is able to be transcended. The experience of such moments of insight, for May, signifies maturity.

Kobasa and Maddi (1977) have attempted to create an existential model, subdivided into early and later development.

Early development

During this time the child is dependent and needs guidance from caregivers to develop courage, or what Maddi and Kobasa (1984) call 'hardiness'. The development of hardiness is supported if caregivers:

1) expose children to rich and diverse experiences,
2) freely impose limits based on their own sense of what is meaningful in life,
3) love and respect their children as budding individuals, and
4) teach the value of vigorous symbolism, imagination and judgement directly by example

(Maddi 1996)

In a climate rich in these experiences the child begins to differentiate 'facticity' (unchangeable givens) from possibility, and tends towards choosing the future and tolerating ontological anxiety, rather than the past with its accompanying ontological guilt about missed opportunity.

Later development

This begins, according to Kobasa and Maddi (1977), when courage has been developed, usually around adolescence. They outline two transitional stages that are passed through before authenticity can be reached. The first of these is the 'aesthetic phase', occurring as soon as the person leaves the family. This phase is the person's first attempt at independence. It is typified by living self-indulgently in the moment and not making any lasting commitments or deep relationships. Maddi describes the way in which the person who has developed courage begins to learn from the loneliness and emptiness of living only in the present, 'what at first seemed like wonderful freedom becomes emptiness' (Maddi 1996).

This person begins to try to account for the past and future in their choice-making by behaving as if present involvements and beliefs are eternal. They thus move on to the 'idealistic phase'. This phase is characterized by uncompromising principles and undying commitments. Such an idealistic orientation inevitably leads to repeated experiences of failure. Again, if courage has developed, these failures represent a developmental opportunity. The idealistic phase comes to an end as the individual learns 'of the limited control people have over events and others' (Maddi 1996).

With this learning, the phase of authenticity begins. Maddi (1996) suggests that this does not occur before middle adulthood. If courage has not been developed then failure is overwhelming and must be defended against rather than learnt from. This is likely to leave an individual dependent and passive.

Conclusions

Existential theorists have not sought to create the kind of models produced by some other orientations outlined in this book. There is, nevertheless, a model of development in as much as there is a picture of what maturity is, and also of how such maturity is achieved. However restrictive the external environment may be, for the existentialist we are always more than the victim of circumstances. By paying attention to the 'givens' of life, we can become more authentically aware of what we are able to influence. Life is considered to be about deciding the personal meaning we derive from life. To quote Frankl (1973: 13),

> in the last resort, man should not ask 'What is the meaning of my life?' but should realise that he himself is being questioned. Life is putting its problems to him, and it is up to him to respond to these questions by being responsible; he can only answer to life by answering *for his* life.
>
> (author's italics)

CHAPTER 5

Moral development

Val Simanowitz

The development of moral thinking, or the way in which moral judgements are made, is a particular area of psychosocial development that has been studied. Lawrence Kohlberg takes the view that one of the major developmental tasks is moral decision-making. In his paper 'Moral stages and moralisation' (1976) and in *The Philosophy of Moral Development* (1981) he develops a theoretical description of six moral stages of development. He attempts to define moral development and follows this by a description of how he found methods for identifying moral stages.

Following the publication of Kohlberg's ideas, Carol Gilligan in *In a Different Voice* (1982) put forward some extremely convincing arguments to show that his moral stages were constructed from a very male perspective and his lower and higher levels of morality were based on a view biased by masculine preconceptions and omitting the female experience.

Lawrence Kohlberg: six stages of moral development

Kohlberg looks at the place of moral development in the overall sequence of personality development. He describes six stages through which people pass, as they progress from the most basic stage – Stage 1 to Stage 6 – although in his book Kohlberg suggests a hypothetical 'Stage 7' (his inverted commas) which is an ideal position, similar to the Platonic Ideal. He considers that the development of our logical reasoning is a necessary condition for moral development. An example of this is that in an undeveloped Turkish village, where people had little opportunity to develop logical reasoning, most people only reached the early stages of moral development.

Table 5.1 Kohlberg's six stages of moral development

Level of judgement	Basis for moral decisions
Pre-conventional	1. Fear
	2. Self-interest
Conventional	3. Conformity
	4. Social order
Post-conventional	5. Rights of others
	6. Universal principles

He also considers that social perspectives are a necessary prerequisite for moral development. Logical development and social perspectives underpin all stages of moral development.

Kohlberg thinks social role-taking is an essential element in forming the person's social perspective. He defines social role-taking as the way one person is able to see another, interpret their thoughts and feelings, and see their place in society. However, though social role-taking is necessary, it is not a sufficient condition for moral development to occur. It also does not usually include a reference point for judging what is right or wrong.

Moral stages are closely related to moral behaviour, and to behave in a morally high way requires 'a high stage of moral reasoning' (Kohlberg 1976: 32). However, people's behaviour does not always live up to the stage they have reached in moral reasoning in any given situation.

Therapists often work with clients' search for identity and thus often engage in existential questions about values and meanings. Clients identify conflicts and discrepancies between their moral principles and behaviour. For example, a client may strongly believe it is wrong to hurt others, particularly those close to her, and so agonize over having an ongoing affair and hurting her husband and children; or a client who believes in keeping society's rules may cheat the benefits agency, perhaps for the sake of her children who are having to go without the toys or clothes that other children around them have. Some reference to Kohlberg's stages of moral development can be a guideline in such cases, although it is equally possible to argue that hierarchical notions of a higher or lower moral developmental stage are not particularly relevant.

Three levels of moral stages: pre-conventional, conventional and post-conventional

Kohlberg bases his research on a longitudinal study (over 12 years) of a group of 84 boys. He perceives three types of relationship levels between a person and society's rules and regulations.

The pre-conventional, level 1 (stages 1 and 2) (see Table 5.1) includes children under 9 years of age, some adolescents and some adult offenders. At that level the person conforms to rules that are external to them. When researchers asked Joe, aged 10 'Why shouldn't you steal from a store?' he answered that it was against the law and that someone could see you and call the police. As far as he was concerned, the only reason for obeying the law was to avoid punishment. He was only considering his own interests.

At level 2 (stages 3 and 4), the conventional level, the person internalizes the rules of society, which become their own, especially when the rules emanate from authority figures. When Joe, aged 17, was asked the same question, 'Why shouldn't you steal from a store?' he again said it was against the law but went on to take some owner-ship of it. 'It's one of our rules, we're trying to protect everyone, protect property . . . if we didn't have these laws society would get out of kilter.' Here Joe is concerned for the good of society as a whole; he is talking about 'us' not just himself.

At level 3 (stages 5 and 6), the post-conventional level, the person can differentiate the self from rules and can define their values in terms of principles they have considered and adopted for themselves. When Joe, aged 24, was asked, 'Why shouldn't someone steal from a store?', he answered, 'It's violating another person's rights, in this case to property'. His answer shows that he is now able to see the perspectives of both the individual and society. There is a moral principle strongly at stake.

Social perspectives: how the two stages differ within each of the three levels

As previously mentioned, there are two stages within each of the three moral levels (the pre-conventional, the conventional and the post-conventional). At each level the second stage represents a pro-gression from the first. The researchers asked the question 'Should you tell your father about your brother's disobedience after he has confided in you?' At level one (stage 1) the 10-year-old answers that he would tell his father for fear he might be beaten. Here he considers only his own interests. At age 13 he says he would not tell because he might get his brother into trouble and that he would want his brother to keep quiet for him in a similar situation. Here the boy has moved from level 1 stage 1 to level 1 stage 2. He has concern for his brother's welfare as well as considering how this affects his own interests.

Or take the different stages at level 3 (post-conventional). Here the respondent is asked about Heinz's dilemma. Heinz's wife is very ill with cancer and he has no money for a drug that could help her. The question asked is 'Would you steal drugs to save your wife's life?' A respondent may answer 'The moral and legal usually coincide but here they conflict. The judge should weigh up the moral standpoint more.' This is a typical stage 5 reaction: the moral value is not yet seen as superseding legal values, so law and morality are, more or less, on an equal footing. The level 3 stage 6 answer takes another step: it concludes, 'treat each person as an end, not a means', and it thus shows a clear awareness of a moral view based on principle.

The distinctive features of moral judgement

Kohlberg attempts to define moral judgement by listing the primary moral categories from which judgement springs. He calls the categories moral orientations and describes four kinds of universal elements to be found in any social situation. These are:

1. The normative order. This shows that the basic consideration in decision-making is related to rules. In answer to 'Why shouldn't you steal from a store?', the answer is 'It's always wrong to break the rules'.
2. The utility consequences. This is related to how an action can affect you or another in a good or bad way. The answer to the stealing question is 'You're hurting other people. The storeowner has a family to support.'
3. Justice or fairness. This is linked to relations of liberty, equality and reciprocity between persons. The answer to why you shouldn't steal from a store is that the storeowner worked hard for his money and you didn't. Therefore why should you have it?
4. The ideal self. This is related to the image of the person as a good self, someone with a conscience moved by motives of virtue, independent of approval from others. The answer to the stealing question is that a person who steals is dishonest.

Kohlberg describes how different philosophers adhere to one or other of these categories. For example, Kant, Durkheim and Piaget identify with adherence to rules; Mills and Dewey have considerations of general welfare. However, Kohlberg himself considers that justice is the most essential structure of morality. 'The core of justice is the distribution of rights and duties regulated by concepts of equality and reciprocity.' (Kohlberg 1976: 40)

Kohlberg and his team claim that anyone who interviews children about moral development over a similar period of time would come to the same conclusions about the six stages of moral development as they did. Kohlberg contends that his methods are not 'contingent on any psychological theory but are matters of logical analysis' (1976: 47). He states that the stages have implications for the many social science theories of moralization and are often in contrast to those theories.

Theories of moral development: cognitive-developmental, socialization and psychoanalytic

The most obvious characteristic of cognitive theory is that moral attitudes develop as people grow older and become more mature. Other common assumptions are that:

1. Moral development has a moral judgement component.
2. The motivation for morality is a generalized motivation for acceptance, competence and self-esteem, not a biological need or way of reducing fear.
3. Basic principles arise through experience of social interaction.
4. Major aspects of moral development are culturally universal.
5. The general quality and extent of social and intellectual stimulation during the child's development constitute environmental influences.

These assumptions are in sharp contrast with the socialization theories of morality, which propose that:

1. Moral development is conformity to moral rules.
2. The basic motives for morality are rooted in biological needs or social reform.
3. Moral development is culturally relative.
4. Environmental influences on development are caused by variations in the richness or severity of the rewards and punishments children

receive and the model of conforming behaviour they see in parents and significant others.

Freudian theory is similar to the socialization theory as it also describes development in stages, but the stages are libidinal-instinctual rather than moral. It shares the belief that that moralization is the internalization of cultural or parental norms. (See chapter one.)

Cognitive theory argues that the stimulation of moral development has a large social component. It comes from social interaction, moral decision-making, moral dialogue and moral interaction. The family provides these opportunities, as does the peer group, school and the child's social status within society. If parents encourage dialogue on issues of value within the home this has been found to have a great influence on moral development and advance. Participation in groups provides the child with an opportunity to see others' perspectives. Mutuality of role-taking within the group is also important. As an example of this, children were studied in an American orphanage and in a kibbutz. The children in the kibbutz had the highest level of moral development and the children in the American orphanage the lowest. Although both groups had little interaction with their parents, the children in the kibbutz had intense interactions with their peers, and were supervised by a good leader. In the orphanage there was little interaction between adult staff and the children.

One boy from the orphanage did not see why promises should be kept. In his experience his mother had promised many times to come and see him and had let him down. Prisons and orphanages are, of course, exceptional environments, but it is plausible that participation in institutions that are run with an ethos that is perceived to be at a much higher moral level than the child's own home environment is a strong component of moral development.

Research by Rest, Turiel and Kohlberg (1969) suggests that adolescents tend to assimilate moral reasoning from those who are older and who appear to have reached a stage above their own. Hickey, Starve and Kohlberg attempt to prove that the creation of a higher stage institutional atmosphere will lead to moral change by developing a 'just community'. This happened in a women's prison, where there had been involvement in community decisions and small group moral discussions. It led to improvements in moral reasoning and changes in lifestyle and behaviour.

Cognitive moral conflict is also an important ingredient in progression to a higher stage of moral development. Conflict can occur when people have to make decisions involving internal contradictions or when they are exposed to a moral reasoning that opposes their own. This principle was observed in moral discussion programmes that Kohlberg implemented in schools.

In a longitudinal study on how people shift from conventional to principled morality, it seemed that the experience of college, with its tendency towards more independence, less authority and exposure to a range of conflicting values, might stimulate such a shift. At college, students were exposed to the questioning of conventional morality: for example, one young officer serving in Vietnam rebelled when he became aware of the conflict between the army morality and the more universal rights of the Vietnamese.

Kohlberg acknowledges that cognitive-developmental theory can seem limited and abstract when we move to the individual life experiences that stimulate moral development. He considers it then becomes useful to look at the individual's ego level as well as their moral stages. Moral development theories are sometimes useful as part of broader theories of emotional development such as Erikson's eight-stage model. However, Kohlberg maintains that moral development should not be treated as simply a facet of ego development. Moral structures often equate to ego development, but moral structures can be found that are distinct from ego development. The moral stages need to be defined more specifically than by the ways used to define ego development.

> To see moral stages as simply reflections of ego-level, however, is to lose the ability to theoretically define and empirically find order in the specifically moral domain of the human personality.
>
> (Kohlberg 1976: 53)

Carol Gilligan's feminist critique of Kohlberg's developmental theory

Carol Gilligan in *In a Different Voice* (1982) develops a strong critique of Kohlberg's theory, and indeed of most psychological developmental or life cycle theories. She points out that most of them are male-orientated, are developed from a male perspective and take the male as the norm. Girls' and women's differing perceptions are seen therefore as deviations from the norm and thus inferior. Life cycle theories are an attempt to order and make clear the unfolding experiences and perceptions, the changing wishes and realities of everyday life. But the nature of such conceptions depends in part on the position of the observer. These observers are predominantly male.

(Gilligan 1982: 152)

Gilligan points out that Kohlberg's research into the moral development of the child was based on studies of 84 boys whom he considered represented the 'norm'. There is an implicit assumption that female deviations are not just different but intrinsically less moral. What is actually a flaw in the research method and the theory is perceived as a flaw in women.

One of Kohlberg's criteria for reaching a higher level of moral development is respect for rules. Whereas Piaget argues that children learn this respect for rules by playing rule-bound games, Kohlberg points out that children learn these rules most effectively by role-taking within such games, while trying to resolve disputes. However, Piaget also points out that there are strong sex differences in the way boys and girls play games and in the kinds of games they play. Boys grow increasingly fascinated with the rules, whereas girls have a pragmatic attitude. They are more tolerant, more willing to make exceptions and more willing to make innovations and changes. As a result a 'legal sense is far less developed in little girls than in boys' (Piaget 1932: 77). Kohlberg concludes that traditional girls' games offer far less opportunity for moral lessons than do boys'. Girls' games, such as hopscotch, are non-competitive and do not need to have a loser. Lever (1976: 482) demonstrates that if a quarrel broke out girls would often end a game, putting their wish to keep friendly relationships before the continuation of the game.

Horner (1968) observes how this lack of competitive urge in girls extends into adulthood. Women in a series of thematic apperception tests (TATS) show considerable anxiety about anything competitive. Many women perceive there to be a conflict between femininity and success. Sassen (1980) observes that inner conflict is exacerbated by 'a heightened perception of the other side of success.' This involves emotional cost and the need for someone else to fail.

There is also a difference in adult men's and women's attitudes to success. The fact that men assess their social orientation by their position and status in the world, whereas woman assess theirs by more personal criteria, such as family relationships, can be traced back to earlier attitudes in play.

Within Kohlberg's system, women's judgements, which conceive morality to be interpersonal and based on connecting with and pleasing others, seem to be an example of the third stage in his six-stage sequence, and thus they do not reach the highest post-conventional levels. This may be because Kohlberg's starting point for his ideas of moral development is Freud's view of a sense of justice (see chapter six). Freud found this to be flawed in women, because they did not accept the concept of 'blind impartiality'.

Kohlberg and Kramer (1973) think that women's lives are limited by the fact that they are confined to the home. They imply that if women were to participate in the traditional male workplace they would recognize how inadequate their moral perspective is and reach a stage in which relationships are subordinated to rules (stage 4) and rules to the universal principle of justice. Lever (1976), too, concludes that boys' competitiveness in play is a much better model for corporate success in adulthood. With women's increasingly high participation in the traditional male workplace, we may wonder how Kohlberg and Kramer would assess their moral perspective now!

Studies of sex role stereotypes (Broverman, Vogel *et al.* 1972) have found that the qualities male psychologists consider necessary for mature adulthood are associated with masculinity. These qualities are autonomous thinking, clear decision-making and responsible action. Expressive capacities are relegated to women. Intimacy, which men are perhaps only now acknowledging as important, has been considered as intuitive or instinctive, and thus, Gilligan suggests (1982: 17), psychologists have failed to describe its development.

Psychologists have, therefore, a problem with understanding the female perspective and translate this into their view that women have problems with development. The 'nature and significance of women's development has been ... obscured and shrouded in mystery' (Gilligan 1982: 18).

Freud, Erikson, Blos and others have seen the ability to separate from parents, usually in adolescence, as positive development and they see failure to separate as failure to develop. They have observed differences in the way male adolescents find it easier to separate than females. But some female analysts and psychologists have an alternative explanation for the differences in women's rates of development and for gender-specific responses to issues of connection and separation. Chodorow (1974) claims that sex differences occur in the personality development of male and female because the primary carer in the first three years of life is usually female (see chapter six).

When Kohlberg and his team asked Jake and Amy (both aged 11

and both intelligent) 'When responsibility to self and others conflicts how should one choose?', Jake answered 'One fourth to others and three fourth to self'; whereas Amy answered, 'It depends on the situation: if you have a responsibility with someone else you should keep it to a certain extent, to the extent that it is going to hurt you or stop you doing something you really want, then I think that maybe you should put yourself first' (Gilligan 1982: 35).

Gilligan points out that Amy's response proceeds from a premise of connection; to her, responsibility is a response rather than a limitation to actions. Amy starts by assuming connections and then explores separation, whereas Jake assumes separation and then explores connection – 'The most important thing in your decisions should be yourself, don't let yourself be guided totally by other people but you should take them into consideration.'

> In view of these different paths of development and particularly of the different ways experiences of separation and development are aligned with the voice of self, the representation of the boy's development as the single line of adolescent development for both sexes creates a continual problem when it comes to interpreting the development of the girl.
>
> (Gilligan 1982: 39)

Kohlberg concludes that girls show a failure to develop to the higher stages of moral decision-making. They have a different attitude to the moral problems posed to them in the research projects, focusing on their responsibilities and relationships rather than on fairness, rights and rules. This is illustrated by the answers in a number of projects ranging across different age groups.

Kohlberg asked Amy and Jake the question about whether Heinz, who had no money, should steal drugs from a pharmacist to save his dying wife. Jake was clear that Heinz should steal the drug; he thought that his wife's life came before theft, and that law was only man-made and the judge would probably consider the stealing right in the circumstances. Amy seemed less able to think for herself and was very hesitant in her answers. She thought Heinz should not steal but also that his wife should not die. Amy thought that Heinz should not steal because it could affect his future relationship with his wife; he might go to jail and therefore be unable to help her when she needed him again. She saw the problem as the pharmacist's failure and thought it would be important to persuade the pharmacist to give the drug.

Amy and Jake perceive fundamentally different moral problems and arrive at different answers. Jake works within systems of logic and law, while Amy sees the problem as rooted in communication and relationship. Amy's assumptions were questioned and the interviewers did not understand her responses as she interpreted questions differently from Jake, answering not 'whether?' but 'how?' Amy was therefore relegated to stage one of moral development, a stage lower than Jake; the interviewers thought her dependence on relationship revealed vulnerability, naivety and immaturity. But in *her* perception of the world, people are responsible to each other and there is an ethic of care. It seems the interviewers missed this aspect in her responses.

Again, when in a different experiment Jake and Amy were asked to describe themselves, Jake set himself apart from the world by his ability, belief and height. He measured himself against an ideal of perfection. Amy, however, defined herself in relation to the world and chose to help others through her science.

Take another example: when interviewers asked two other children, Karen and Jeffrey (aged 8), about a conflict between desire and duty, Jeffrey said he thought about the 'right thing to do'. What was right was his priority. Karen, however, chose to play with a lonely friend above the others, as she focused on the one who was left out.

> Two views of morality one focussing on hierarchy and the other on network are different but complementary rather than opposed. But this construction of differences goes against the bias of developmental theory towards ordering differences in a hierarchical mode.
>
> (Gilligan 1982: 33)

From answers given by two educated and intelligent 25-year-olds, one male, one female, to some questions about the nature of morality, Kohlberg perceives the male as having reached the highest stages (stages 5 and 6) because he moves 'to a perspective outside that of his society'. He identifies morality with justice (fairness, rights, the golden rule), with recognition of the rights of others (Kohlberg 1976: 29–30). The woman's answer is not based on the primacy of rights but on a 'very strong sense of being responsible to the world'. Kohlberg's conception of rights is geared to arriving at objectivity, at a fair and just resolution of moral dilemmas. The woman's responsibility concept shows that any resolutions have limitations and that conflicts remain.

Unlike Kohlberg, Gilligan considers that women's moral judgements are an alternative conception of maturity, not a lesser one. She
finds evidence that women find safety in relationships and intimacy,
whereas men find them dangerous. On the other hand, women
find danger in impersonal achievement situations that result in
competitive success.

In a survey of college students (Pollak and Gilligan 1982), the
researchers observe that male and female students interpreted pictures in different ways, very much along gender lines. Students were
shown a picture of a tranquil scene showing a couple sitting by a
bench. Gilligan observed that 21 per cent of 88 men in the class had
projected images of violence onto the scene, but none of the 50
women in the class had done so.

Again, when the same students were shown a picture of two trapeze
artists grasping each other's wrists, the man hanging by his knees
from the trapeze and the woman in mid-air, the men often saw violence in the scene and the women focused on safety. Twenty-two per
cent of the women added nets. By providing nets they had made the
scene safe. Men interpreted the female responses as denying danger or
repressing aggression. Through their care, women think they can
make their social world safe. The prevalence of violence in men's
fantasies and the fact that they sensed danger everywhere reveals a
problem in making connections. Male psychologists, instead of inter-
preting women's responses as problems with separation might also
interpret them as men's problems with connection!

Women psychologists, psychiatrists, therapists and researchers
have drawn attention to the fact that because women's experience is
different it is considered inferior, or women are thought to have
reached a lower stage of development. However, often there is no
language with which to assess their difference. Jean Baker Miller
suggests that 'the parameters of female development are not the same
as the male's and that the same terms do not apply' (1976: 86). She
finds there is no language to describe how women's sense of self is
'organised around being able to make and maintain affiliations
and relationships' (Baker 1976: 83). Consequently, when female
realities are questioned or negated, when nets are seen as entrapments
rather than protections against falling, women question their own
experience.

> Personal doubts invade their sense of themselves, compromising
> their ability to act on their own perceptions. This issue becomes
> central in women's adolescent years when thought becomes

reflective and the problem of interpretation enters the stream of development itself.

(Gilligan 1982: 49)

For example, Claire, a participant in the college study, was asked to describe herself when in her senior year at college. Her answer was 'confused' . . . 'I am more unsure now than I think I have ever been'. She thought that people's perceptions of her were different from her own and felt caught in the middle: 'All these various roles just aren't exactly right'. She found it hard to identify 'What is right for me' and tried to explain herself as both separated and connected.

Margaret Warner (1999) stresses that the language of psychological theory is disempowering to women: 'Psychological theories are, of course intended to be personally empowering. However, in psychological speaking and writing the structure of language itself often implies that a single externally validated reality exists which is applicable to all groups' (Warner 1999: 196). She writes 'Psychologists . . . need to present their views as opinions they hold for some reasons rather than implying that they are value neutral entities which have an independent existence in the world' (1999: 198).

A 20-year-old client Marion exemplifies Gilligan's view of how women's perceptions of their own development are marred by male criteria. She comes to counselling because her self-esteem is very low. She is very timid, speaks quietly and finds it difficult to function in ordinary social situations like the pub. In her family, her older brother was valued above her and her mother would give him full attention on his return from school, while ignoring Marion's chatter. She is grieving because her first and only boyfriend has decided that he wants to end the relationship and has found another girlfriend. After some initial wariness she felt very close to him and let down her guard despite her usual problems with trust. However, the fulfilment she found through this closeness has now evaporated and turned to disillusion.

The therapist finds it really difficult to help Marion to value her positive qualities. She is caring and compassionate towards family and friends and she is deeply concerned with environmental issues. She has eight GCSEs and two A levels with good grades but does not rate either her personal qualities or her obvious academic ability. She compares herself unfavourably with her brother, who is studying engineering. She is working in a dead-end job in an office and spends every evening at home watching TV with her parents. When she tries to express her thoughts and feelings, she says she 'cannot find the words'. She feels her contribution is of no interest or value.

As the sessions progress, the therapist finds Gilligan's identification of the low status given to female qualities such as compassion, compared with the high status accorded to male success (her brother's ability at maths and science subjects), is a useful starting point in understanding Marion's situation. Shared with Marion, it may enable her to gain insight into some of the roots of her sense of inferiority and thus to begin to develop her self-esteem and her sense of identity and to realize her potential.

The human paradox

Gilligan highlights the fact that women's experience provides

> a non-hierarchical vision of human connection. Since relationships when cast in the image of hierarchy appear inherently unstable and morally problematic, their transposition on to the image of a web changes an order of inequality not a structure of interconnection.
>
> (Gilligan 1982: 62)

Although psychological theory has devalued women's experience as compared to that of the male, Gilligan asserts that both the web and the hierarchy are embedded in the cycle of all human life: 'We know ourselves as separate only insofar as we live in connection with others and we experience relationship only insofar as we differentiate others from self' (Gilligan 1982: 63). What is important is not that we separate out the male and the female psychologists' versions of moral development, and see them as conflicting – as perhaps the men might do – but that, as the women would prefer, we see them as essentially related, each one expressing important values in the movement towards maturity.

CHAPTER 6

Feminist critiques of developmental theories

Val Simanowitz

In therapy, women clients share a number of common themes: low self-esteem, lack of confidence, a tremulous sense of identity, depression, and relationship problems; many of these issues arise from emotional, physical or sexual abuse from family or partners.

Women's experience during their early developmental years is often distinctively different from that described in the best-known developmental theories; and this can be ascribed to the fact that usually a woman's perspective has not been acknowledged nor has her voice been heard.

However, the rise of feminism in the 1970s stimulated numerous critiques of these theories, targeting Freudian psychoanalysis, Kleinian object relations and Eriksonian ego psychology. For the first time women thinkers, theorists and therapists were able to articulate and demonstrate how theories written from a male perspective perpetuated gender inequality in society. Part of the problem lay in the traditional presumption that the gender roles of the heterosexual nuclear family were the 'norm', and indeed that qualities often associated with the male were also superior, for example independence.

We can see now that women therapists themselves unconsciously internalized some of these sexist ideologies and in effect reinforced the old gender roles. Later, even these feminist revisionists had to seriously consider whether *their* new conclusions might strengthen not only sexual but also race and class divisions.

However, it is undoubtedly true that many therapists, both male and female, have had to revise their thinking as a result of well-reasoned, clear and original arguments, as well as the high status of the writers, notably Nancy Chodorow and Carol Gilligan (both university professors). In therapy they face their clients from a new perspective, trying to ensure they give equal consideration to both female and male development.

In this chapter we examine some critiques of the developmental concepts of both Freud and Klein, as well as of Erikson's ego psychology, and of Daniel Levinson's and George Vaillant's descriptions of the stages of male development.

Dorothy Dinnerstein, Nancy Chodorow, Jessica Benjamin, Susie Orbach and Leslie Eichenbaum are all feminist object relations therapists who accept Klein's emphasis on the significance of the mother–daughter relationship and go on to bring a feminist perspective to the creation of new developmental models. Gilligan brings a different and female voice to Erikson's eight-stage theory of human (basically male) development. In a similar way she re-evaluates Levinson's and Vaillant's studies of life stages, which focus on work and success as the greatest life achievement.

Freud and penis envy

Feminists have long been outraged by the male bias and assumption of male superiority evident in Freud's work. Kate Millett describes him as 'the strongest counterrevolutionary force in the ideology of sexual politics' (1969: 178). Some of Freud's ideas on human development have been discussed in chapter one. His emphasis on the little girl's penis envy has been particularly criticized by feminists: 'She has seen it and knows that she is without it and wants to have it' (Freud 1925: 188).

Freud sees the consequences of penis envy as part of woman's inferiority, as a stimulus to excessive female jealousy, as the cause of loosening her ties with her mother, whom she blames: 'as the reason for a girl replacing her wish for a penis with a wish for a child, taking her father as love object, and as a reason why the girl must eliminate clitoral sexuality as a precondition for true femininity' (Freud 1925: 191).

These views have led to unfortunate consequences (although not always intended by Freud) such as contempt for women; and the view of the male as active (the subject) and the female as passive (the object). It is clear from his conclusions that Freud took the male as normal and the female as diverging from the normal.

In his 1925 essay Freud develops his theory of penis envy to identify what he considered to be the difference in the superego (conscience and a sense of morality) in boys and girls. He says that in boys the Oedipus complex

> is smashed to pieces by fear of castration and is replaced by conscience and morality. However in girls the fear of castration is lacking thus the Oedipus complex only disappears gradually, if at all ... I cannot escape the notion (though I hesitate to give it expression) that for women the level of what is ethically normal is different from what it is in men ... Character traits which critics of every epoch have brought up against women – that they show less sense of justice than men, that they are less ready to submit to the great necessities of life, that they are more often influenced in their judgement by feelings of affection or hostility – all these would be amply accounted for by the modification in the formation of their superego which we have already inferred.

The vast majority of crimes of violence – murder, robbery, incest and rape – are committed by men, and there are disproportionately larger numbers of men in prison (the prison population of the UK in 2002 was 69,847 of which female prisoners account for 4208, about 6 per cent). Most known domestic abusers are men; men are largely responsible for white-collar crimes; and it is principally men who are responsible for initiating, perpetuating and undertaking war and its atrocities. It is therefore ironic that Freud should suggest that women have 'less sense of justice'. Such an indubitably false opinion must largely be ascribed to his own male bias.

Freud considers that a man aged 30 is 'youthful' and capable of making 'powerful use of the possibilities for development offered up to him by analysis'. A woman of the same age is often beyond help: '[she] frightens us by her psychic rigidity and unchangeability ... there are no paths open to further development'. Charlotte Prozan is shocked by Freud's apparent acceptance of this situation and lack of desire to challenge it. Perhaps again we can ascribe this to the deep-seated sexist influences of his background and culture. Prozan considered that Freud's thinking was strongly affected by three main influences: the Catholic Church and its influence on the philosophy of medical science at the time; the influence of Judaism; and his family background (Prozan 1992: 20). The attitude to women in the Vienna of Freud's time was certainly conducive to male superiority. In 1867 a law was passed preventing females, foreigners and minors from engaging in any political activity. A woman had to recognize her husband as head of the family and obey his orders; and women who sought education were scorned (Gay 1988: 510). It is not surprising that Freud did not permit Martha Bernays, who became his wife, to work.

The medical profession had long been deeply misogynist, and in the Middle Ages (fourteenth to seventeenth centuries) colluded with the burning of large numbers of witches, who were feared for their ability as lay healers. Women were relegated to the role of subordinates in the medical profession and were not allowed to study in medical school. Freud prevented his own daughter Anna from studying at medical school (though he did allow her to train as an analyst).

Evelyn Fox Keller (1985) observes that science 'casts objectivity, reason and mind as male and subjectivity, feeling and nature as female' and that science 'the province of the impersonal and rational and general has been the preserve of men'. In the light of this knowledge we can better understand the attitude of early medical scientists and the 'unfortunate conclusions drawn by Freud and supported by his co-workers on the inferiority of women' (Prozan 1992: 6). But even if this background is not something for which Freud can be held responsible, the culture must surely have influenced the way he interpreted what he was hearing from his female patients.

Although Freud was not a practising Jew, he acknowledged a strong Jewish identity; and he was indubitably influenced by some of the misogynist concepts of that culture. These concepts include the inferior status of women, apparent from their segregation in the synagogue, their absence in the performance of religious ritual (a service can only begin if ten men are present) and the daily prayer uttered by men 'Thank God for making me a man and not a woman'. He may have been influenced by such strictures from the Talmud as, 'And talk not over much with women-for by such talk man brings evil upon himself.' It is possible that Freud's view of women, as having less sense of justice and being less ethical than men, also originated in Judaism.

However, for all that, we also have to remember that women flourished more obviously in the second phase of the psychoanalytic movement than they did in many allied professions. The list of women psychoanalytic writers is impressive: Anna Freud, Dorothy Burlingham, Melanie Klein, Helene Deutsch, Lou Andreas-Salome, Joan Riviere, Jeanne Lampl-de Groot, to mention only those who were influential from the 1920s onwards. But, of course, it could be argued that many of their views were closely tied to Freud's.

Critiques of psychoanalytic and object relations developmental theories: Dorothy Dinnerstein, Nancy Chodorow and Jessica Benjamin

Although it was only in the 1970s and with the rise of feminism that critiques of analytical theory began to be taken seriously, Karen Horney had challenged Freud 40 years earlier.

She was an analyst and lecturer at the Berlin Psychoanalytic Institute in the 1920s, and had already challenged tradition by breaking away from the conventional life path prescribed for women of her day. In 1917 she wrote a paper challenging some of the Freudian views on the unconscious. In some later writing she concentrated on *woman's* nature and refused to agree with Freud's contention that femininity is essentially acquired by successive renunciation of masculine traits (Gay 1988: 519). At the Psychoanalytic Congress in Berlin in 1922 Horney suggested a revised theory of penis envy. She thought it existed but that it was part of 'normal female development, it was not a creator of femininity but an expression of it'. She suggested that it was masculine narcissism that led psychoanalysts to believe that women reject their femaleness (Prozan 1992: 71).

Horney emphasized the importance of motherhood and claimed that the little boy had 'an intense envy of motherhood'. During her analysis of her male patients she noticed the intensity of 'this envy of pregnancy, childbirth and motherhood as well as of the breasts and of the act of suckling'. (1922) Thus she placed the focus on *womb envy* rather than penis envy. She went on to claim that it was men's unconscious need to depreciate motherhood and see it as a burden that arose from this earlier envy.

However, not surprisingly, Freud dismissed Horney's contributions and at the same time sought to disparage her as an analyst so that his views reigned supreme. 'We shall not be so very greatly surprised if a woman analyst who has not been sufficiently convinced of the intensity of her own desire for a penis also fails to assign adequate importance to that factor in her patients' (Kelman 1967: 26).

After Horney emigrated to the USA (in the 1930s) she appears to have turned away from an interest in feminine psychology. She was involved in various splits with the psychoanalytic establishment of her day, which left her in despair. She died of cancer in 1953, not living to see the revival of her work by the women's movement.

Melanie Klein, like Horney, published articles between 1927 and 1935, questioning Freud's theories of female developmental psychology. As Klein's developmental theories have been described elsewhere in this book (chapter one), we concentrate on her emphasis on the mother–daughter relationship, which formed the basis for feminist critiques by object relations theorists and therapists, such as Dinnerstein (1976), Chodorow (1978), Benjamin (1988) and Janine Chasseguet-Smirgel (1970).

These feminist analysts sought to integrate the values and knowledge acquired from feminist studies into the canon of psychoanalysis. They attempted 'to correct the errors within psychoanalysis and create a new psychology of women for the sake of those patients who continued to come to analysis and whose symptoms and needs can be better treated by means of this integration'. At the same time there has been a focus on what men are missing, particularly in the areas of emotion and intimacy (Prozan 1992: 99). *Female Sexuality: New Psychoanalytic Views* by Chasseguet-Smirgel, for example, contains six papers by Kleinians with extensive clinical material focusing on the infant–mother relationship during the first year of life. They stress how the mother–child relationship influences feminine personality and all future sexual developments.

Dorothy Dinnerstein, a psychologist of Rutgers University, wrote one of the earliest books of this genre, *The Mermaid and the Minotaur* (1976). In it she focuses on the power of the mother in the infancy and childhood of both men and women. The mother of infancy is a 'magically powerful goddess', the source of ultimate distress as well as ultimate joy. Influenced by Klein, she thinks we all feel ambivalent towards women because

> Like nature she is both nourishing and disappointing, both alluring and threatening, both comforting and unreliable. The infant loves her touch, warmth, shapes, taste and movement . . . and it hates her because, like nature she does not perfectly provide for it
> (Dinnerstein 1976: 95)

'Most men believe in their right to rule the world and most women feel a willingness to let them' (Dinnerstein 1976: 210). Dinnerstein says women are willing to comply with this because of the crucial psychological fact that both men and women fear the will of women. She believes that men have a basic need to 'contain, harness and control' women's power, and for them this is a vital task.

Woman is the first adversary:

> In our first real contest of will we find ourselves more often than not, defeated . . . Power of this kind, concentrated in one sex and

exerted at the outset over both, is far too potent and dangerous a force to be allowed free sway in adult life, To contain it, to keep it under control and harness it to chosen purposes, is a vital need, a vital task, for every mother raised human.

(Dinnerstein 1976: 161)

Dinnerstein does not reject the psychoanalytic insights of Freud and Klein into the importance of childhood, but she enhances them with a 'feminist analysis of how the mother's power in childhood creates the need to diminish women – This was something Freud completely missed' (Prozan 1992: 102). The result of this is a sexual double standard, which carried to its logical conclusion results in man's world-making monopoly. Dinnerstein concludes that woman has been excluded from history because of her status as representative of the flesh, which disqualifies her from participating in our 'communal defiance of the flesh, in our collective counter-assertion to carnality and mortality' (Dinnerstein 1976: 210). However, women have also colluded in their exclusion. Dinnerstein puts their compliance down to two main factors: 'socially sanctioned existential cowardice and motherhood' (1976: 211).

She also believes that the interdependence of men and women has contributed to men's power and women's acquiescence to it. She says that man's right to aggressive actions and woman's exclusive reign over the world of intimacy allow each to express a part for the other, and to experience their own needs through it, in a way that satisfies them both but also deprives them of part of themselves (Prozan 1992: 103).

Woman's role as mother leads to the blaming of all mothers, all women, and eventually to the little girl's self-blame. Women are made the scapegoats for all the ills of life, for their children's psychological difficulties, for schizophrenia, for male impotence, for all forms of neurosis. Women are expected to continue the understanding and tolerance they showed to infants and children, accepting and forgiving everybody's faults while their own are unforgivable. Tammy Wynette's song 'Stand by your man' expresses this perfectly, as the woman permits his infidelity and forgives him because he is 'just a man' (Prozan 1992: 104).

Dinnerstein offers a remedy to this unequal situation in the joint parenting of the young by both men and women. She says that women's faults impinge on the children when they are young and helpless, but men's faults are more remote and forgivable because they are not present in the home. She says there is a need 'for male imperfection to impinge on all of us when we are tiny and helpless so that it becomes as culpable as female imperfection' (1976: 227–38). Her model of human development, while employing psychoanalytical insights, offers an alternative view of the male and female psyche that is not based on penis envy. Indeed, what she does instead is to say that it is the mother, not the penis, that is the source of male anxiety. Hers is a convincing exposition of how men came to dominate society and how women permitted this. It remains to be seen whether the children of those who have taken up shared parenting will live out their genders in different ways, or whether the influence of culture is even stronger than that of the individual family.

In *Towards a New Psychology of Women* (1976) Jean Baker Miller emulates Dinnerstein's focus on the mother–daughter relationship. Miller, a Sullivanian analyst, attributes women's qualities to cultural messages and suppression. She focuses on the subordination of women and the effects of this unequal relationship on both men and women. She points out how subordinates are supposed to fit their roles by being passive and docile and by pleasing others; that those who follow this norm are considered well adjusted but those who do not are considered abnormal. Women who rebel and state their needs are accused of being aggressive and are warned that they will never attract a man and will face an isolated adulthood and old age.

However, Miller sees some strengths arising from this situation: they are, paradoxically, weakness, helplessness and vulnerability but also emotionality, an ability to foster the growth of others, and a sense of cooperation and creativity. She asserts that women have been encouraged to foster the growth of others at the expense of their own growth. She gives a cultural explanation for men's strength, saying that it has been women's role to voice weakness, so that men can continue to deny it. She says that women are conditioned to believe in men's strength, and she does not put their weakness down to 'penis envy'. Miller does not believe that women have to remain weak. They only lack the 'life long belief' that they have a right to in the real world (Prozan 1992: 107–8).

In 1979, inspired by this work, Miller and a group of clinicians set up the Stone Centre for Developmental Studies at Wellesley College, Massachusetts. They were particularly interested in the role of empathy in women's relationships and advanced the notion of 'self in relation' as a means of understanding the psychology of women, particularly the high incidence of depression in women. The group functions, in a cooperative setting, 'relationally and collaboratively' where works in progress are discussed among the membership. Many interesting papers have resulted from the project (Surrey 1990; Kaplan 1990; Jordan 1990).

Nancy Chodorow, in *The Reproduction of Mothering* (1978), also focuses on the centrality of mothering. She was a professor at the Department of Sociology at Berkeley University and is one of the leading theorists in reformulating psychoanalytic developmental theory from a feminist perspective. Unlike other developmental theorists, she takes the experience of women as the central focus and finds it meaningful in itself, not only in how it differs from men's experience.

Like Dinnerstein, Chodorow sees women's mothering as the most important element in the social construction of gender, of male dominance and of women's subordination. She continues in the tradition of Karen Horney and refutes the psychoanalytic theories of female deficiency. She asks questions such as 'How do women today come to mother?' and 'How might we change things to transform the sexual division of labour in which women mother?' (1978: 4). The contemporary reproduction of mothering occurs through social, structurally induced, psychological processes. It is neither the product of biology nor of intentional role training.

> . . . Women as mothers produce daughters with mothering capacities and the desire to mother. These capacities and needs are built into and grow out of the mother daughter relationship itself. By contrast women as mothers produce sons whose nurturing capacities and needs have been systematically curtailed and repressed. This prepares men for their less affective family role . . .
>
> (Chodorow 1978: 7)

Chodorow's view of the Oedipus complex differs radically from Freud's. She believes all infants, both boys and girls, are closely attached to and dependent upon their mothers. Males have to extricate themselves from this attachment in order to become men and enter the male culture: with this comes a major emotional loss. Girls, on the other hand, do not need to detach themselves from their mothers to become women. They learn to become women by remaining closely connected to their mothers. Thus women can tolerate dependence in their lives whereas men are threatened by it. Men find intimacy difficult whereas women have more difficulties with separation. Mothers are more likely to experience their daughters as extensions of themselves, which can lead to boundary problems.

Chodorow challenges the classic psychoanalytic developmental theory that girls change their love allegiance as a result of an erotic turning towards the father. She contends that the girl retains her strong emotional attachment to her mother while her father remains psychologically and physically distant. As she matures, the girl continues to rely on her mother and uses her as a role model for her identification as a woman. The girl attempts to lessen the ties to her mother by love for her father, but he is still a more distant and idealized figure (Prozan 1992: 126).

Chodorow maintains that many relationship problems between heterosexual couples are a result of the fact that men grow up having to reject their need for love and thus find it threatening to have to meet a partner's emotional needs. Thus men both want and fear intimacy with women. 'The relationship to the mother thus builds itself directly into contradictions in masculine heterosexual commitment' (1976: 244). She believes that women are more important to both men and women than men are. When a woman gives birth, the child completes the relationship triangle of childhood, as well as recreating the exclusive mother–child relationship of her own infancy. This is usually recreated for men by a heterosexual relationship. Thus men's lack of emotional availability and women's lesser emotional commitment to the exclusive heterosexual relationship after the advent of a child helps to ensure women's mothering.

Jackie illustrates how men's incapacity to relate emotionally can affect their partners and their children. She is also affected by her mother's 'reproduction of mothering'. She is a married woman in her early 30s, depressed and with low self-esteem. She suffered from the lack of emotional availability in her father, her lover and her husband, as well as from her mother's sex-role stereotyping. Her father was cold and rejecting, and undervalued her warmth and capacity to relate well to others. He could not understand her devastation and depression when he separated from her mother when she was 12. Her first love relationship was disastrous in that she met a man who could not express his feelings and who perceived her love as suffocating; this led to further low self-esteem. Her mother did not value her considerable intellectual abilities, and though she was encouraged to do A levels by her teachers, her mother made her leave school and do office work 'suitable for a girl until she marries'. Her current partner, a 'decent bloke' is totally unable to express feelings or meet her emotional needs.

Chodorow sees men's involvement in the world of work and the public sphere as a way to separate from the pull of women and to avoid dependence and attachment.

> Woman as mother is a fundamental organisational feature of the sex–gender system: it is basic to the sexual division of labour and generates a psychology and ideology of male dominance as well as an ideology of women's capacities and nature. Social reproduction is thus asymmetrical.
>
> (Chodorow 1976: 208–9)

Women in their role of mothers and housewives 'reproduce themselves as mothers, emotionally and psychologically in the next generation'.

Chodorow's answer to the sexual division of labour and sexual inequality is like Dinnerstein's, and involves shared parenting. She thinks such an involvement would also help avoid the psychological fallout of women's over-involvement with their children.

However, Tong (1989), writing from a feminist perspective, high-lights three flaws in the concept of shared parenting. 'First, that it elevates men to the position of saviours; second, that it presupposes that "men pick up all the wondrous feminine qualities previously denied them": third, that women do not pick up any of the horrendous male qualities previously spared them.' (1989: 158–9)

In recent years there have also been critiques of theories of gendered psychological development and parenting as historically and culturally specific accounts of the eurocentric, white middle-class family. Ironically a theory that seeks to get away from male gender bias is now being accused of similar bias against the working class and black/ethnic minority groups.

In *Feminism and Psychoanalytic Theory* (1989) Chodorow again tries to bridge the gap between sociologists, psychoanalysts and feminism. However, in the intervening ten years since her first book, and strongly influenced by the writing of Hans Loewald, she has concluded that psychoanalytical theory has greater significance than other sociological and cultural theories in enabling us to understand the development of female and male gender identity. She says 'I would not, as I believe I do in *Reproduction*, give a determinist primacy to social relations … but would argue that psychology itself is equally important to, constitutive and determinative of, human life.' (1989: 7)

Chodorow contends that there has been a global shift in her general view of feminist theory. She says that her earlier book *The*

Reproduction of Mothering 'implied that women's mothering was *the* cause or prime mover of male dominance. I would now argue that these writings delineate *one* extremely important, and previously unexamined aspect of the relations of gender and the psychology of gender.' (1989: 7) She says that her focus on the pre-Oedipal rather than the Oedipal stage of development was a reaction to a nearly exclusive Freudian focus on the father. However, she says she has yet to find an explanation of 'the virulence of masculine anger, fear and resentment of women that bypasses the psychoanalytic account, first suggested by Horney, that men resent and fear women because they experience them as powerful mothers' (1989: 8).

In the preface to her later book Chodorow claims that her emphasis on the power of the mother does not exclude the recognition of the father's social, cultural and political power. Fathers are not only socially and culturally dominant: they can be personally domineering, seductive and exciting, often as an alternative to the taken-for-granted mother (1989: 7). The general thrust of these essays is that they still argue strongly 'for the necessity to include psychoanalytic understanding, broadly construed, in feminist theory and also feminist understanding, broadly construed in psychoanalysis' (1989: 13–14).

Eichenbaum and Orbach (1983) and Jessica Benjamin (1988) have as feminist therapists used Chodorow as a basis to pose their own questions. For example, how do women still have 'the need to maintain aspects of traditional roles which continue even in the face of strong ideological shifts?' (Chodorow 1978: 33–4).

Although Benjamin identifies the mother–infant relationship as central, she points out that her interest in it differs from Chodorow's. She focuses on the tenacity and dualism of the dynamics of domination and submission in heterosexual relationships. She thinks the appeal of domination lies in the possibility it offers to break out of an isolated sense of self. This isolation arises out of a differentiation between self and other, which is encouraged by the current idealization of masculinity and its conflation with autonomy. She says that what lies behind relations of power between men and women is a longing for recognition that is not possible in a society that refutes dependence.

Heterosexual male domination is an attempt to deny dependency, while the female's desire for submission is a desire for recognition *through male power*. Benjamin is also concerned with how power structures in society reproduce relationships of domination. She contends that psychoanalytic theory has contributed to the notion that male heterosexual domination is natural. She criticizes psychoanalytic theorists' approach to the Oedipal stage of development, which they see as the most crucial stage because it involves detaching from the mother in order to enter a three-sided relationship involving the father. Orthodox psychoanalysts view the crucial dynamic of the Oedipal phase as the father's capacity to *flee the engulfing mother*. Thus, for them, autonomy has come to represent the father, who provides a means of escape from the mother (Heenan and Seu 1998: 102–3).

Eichenbaum and Orbach also build on Chodorow's views on the reproduction of mothering. Men's incapacity to relate leads to a situation where women's emotional needs are not met by their male partners, and so they often turn to their daughters to meet those emotional needs. 'The daughter becomes involved in a cycle, which is part of each woman's experience, attempting to care for mother. As the daughter learns her role as nurturer, her first child is her mother.' (1983: 39) Eichenbaum and Orbach suggest that mothers are confronted with a paradox when raising their daughters. They must meet the dependency needs of their infants while being emotionally undernourished themselves; and they must socialize their daughters for their role in society. Thus daughters too are taught to curb their needs.

Tara, a doctor, is depressed because her image of herself is of someone bad and selfish. She is a devout Christian and her poor self-concept is reinforced by her Church's teaching of the need to abnegate self in the interests of others. She spent most of her childhood trying to please a demanding mother who lent on her heavily for physical and emotional support. She cannot acknowledge that she has needs and rights of her own. Her mother had socialized her for the role of carer, and as a wife and mother herself she felt she fell far short of this.

Later theorists also suggest that although feminist object relations thinkers see heterosexuality as problematic they still accept it as a universalistic concept (O'Connor and Ryan 1993).

We have already referred to Carol Gilligan, a psychologist and Harvard professor, and her critique of Kohlberg in chapter five. However, some of her further work provides a feminist perspective on psychoanalytic and ego psychology developmental theory. Her book *In a Different Voice* has had a greater impact than most feminist/analytical treatises, as it is readily accessible to the reading public and had sold over 450,000 copies by 1992.

Gilligan threw out Freud's theory that women have a weaker super-ego, her main thesis being that for boys and men not playing fair is the worst sin while for girls and women hurting people is the worst sin (see chapter five).

> Sensitivity to the needs of others and the assumption of responsibility for taking care leads women to attend to voices other than their own and to include in their judgement other points of view. Women's moral weakness, manifest in an apparent diffusion and confusion of judgement is thus inseparable from women's moral strength, an overriding concern with relationships and responsibilities.
>
> (Gilligan 1982: 16–17)

Her complaint against psychologists is that they have not listened to, or valued, the voice of caring that is associated with women. They have assumed that male life is the norm and that women's differences and deviations from that norm are consequently inferior. The flaw in their theory is seen as a flaw in women (Prozan 1992: 138).

In the mid-1970s Gilligan taught a course at Harvard University on Erikson's life cycle. She claimed that Erikson bases his theory of eight-stage psychosocial development specifically on the *male* child. In stage 5 (adolescence), for example, Erikson considers that identity precedes intimacy. For Erikson the focus of the latter stage must be individuation – 'the celebration of the autonomous, initiating industrious self' (Gilligan 1982: 12). According to Erikson the sequence is different for the female. Her identity cannot be established until marriage, when she fuses with her husband, so for a woman intimacy precedes identity. In Erikson's view, attachments are hindrances to development, which resonates with Chodorow's description of the male fear of regression to maternal closeness.

Gilligan points out that many psychologists in their developmental theories focus on the self in relation to work. Levinson (see chapter two) sets out on the basis of an all-male study 'to create an over-arching conception of development that could encompass the diverse biological, psychological and social changes occurring in adult life' (Levinson 1978: 8). Levinson's concept is influenced by the idea of 'the dream': a vision of 'glorious achievement whose realization or modification will shape the character of the life of man' (Gilligan 1982: 152). Levinson considers that there are two people who will help the man to realize this dream. These are the 'mentor' and the 'special woman' (Levinson 1978: 93).

Gilligan contends that Levinson sees these people as 'a means to the end of individual achievement who must be cast off or reconstructed following the realization of success' (1982: 152). If they interfere with the realization of the dream they must be rejected. If there seems a danger that the man will not individuate successfully then the man must break out to salvage his dream. The breaking out can be expressed through separation 'leaving his wife, quitting his job, or moving to another region' (Levinson 1978: 206). Thus, 'the road to mid-life salvation runs through the achievement of separation'. To Gilligan it seems that in Levinson's account, relationships play a minor role in the drama of adult development (1982: 152).

There is also a focus on work in George Vaillant's study (1977). The study consist of interviews with men about work, health, stress, death and family relationships, and it is significant that Vaillant says to the men that the hardest question he will ask is 'Can you describe your wife?' He sees occupation as the most significant factor in life and he calls for an expansion in Erikson's stages. He thinks Erikson neglects the decade between the 20s and the 40s. He himself describes the 30s as the years of 'Career Consolidation, when men in his research sought 'the bauble reputation' (1977: 202). Vaillant reinterprets Erikson's stage 7 (adulthood: generativity versus stagnation) to emphasize the importance of the relations of men to society and to minimize attachment to others.

Gilligan points out that it is interesting that in Erikson's, Levinson's and Vaillant's developmental studies 'models for a healthy life style are men who seem distant in their relationships' (1982: 154).

Gilligan contends that in young adulthood the relationship between self and other and issues of identity and intimacy are salient. Theories of human development often fail to show that men's and women's experience of these issues varies considerably. They omit to mention that 'male and female voices speak of the importance of different truths, the former of the role of separation as it defines and empowers the self, the latter of the ongoing process of attachment that creates and sustains the human community'. Gilligan perceives that in these studies the silence of women distorts the narrative of adult development, including its stages and sequences. (1982: 156)

In *Daughtering and Mothering* (1992) Gilligan and Rogers describe a research project they carried out with pre-adolescent and adolescent girls over three years. The project was an exploration of the relationship between pre-adolescent and adolescent daughters and their mothers. Gilligan and Rogers conclude that the relationship between daughters of this age and their mothers is deeply significant. It is greatly affected by the fact that it is at this point that both mothers and daughters begin to withhold the expression of true thoughts and feelings.

For daughters this covering over or avoidance of the truth can feel like a form of betrayal. As girls approach adolescence they show a healthy resistance to what is expected of them. They are unprepared to lose their voices or (as so often happens) to replace their authentic relationships with their mothers with the inauthentic one that often develops around this stage of life. 'For women, joining girls' healthy resistance and recovering the courage to speak one's mind by telling all one's heart' is often in tension with psychological and political pressures to subvert girls' voices and in essence maintain the status quo. This subversion, which constitutes a deeply felt loss in women's development, 'often leaves a residue of bitterness in its wake' (Gilligan and Rogers 1992: 126).

An insistent theme throughout Gilligan's writing is that psycho-logical models of human development are deeply flawed if they leave out the voices of women. A recognition of differences in women's experience and understanding expands our vision of maturity and points to the contextual nature of developmental truths. Through this expansion in perspective we can begin to envision how a marriage between adult development as it is currently portrayed and women's development as it begins to be seen could lead to a changed understanding of human development and a more generative view of human life (Gillian 1982: 174).

Feminist critiques of humanistic developmental theory

As we pointed out in chapter three, humanistic theories do not follow such structured lines as behavioural or psychodynamic theories, although they too are underpinned by developmental themes. There are very few feminist critiques of humanistic theory, but Jocelyn Chaplin in *Feminism and Psychotherapy* (1998: 144) says that some of the more common concepts are open to feminist scrutiny. She says that the focus on a single, unitary self – self-contained, self-directed and self-motivated – can be neglectful of the complex relationship between the self and the socioeconomic, cultural and political forces of society. This can lead to the acceptance by theorists of hidden patterns of domination and hierarchies and to naïve individualism.

She also claims that some humanist developmental theory is itself intrinsically hierarchical, seeing the development of the self proceeding from a low to a 'higher' position. Such concepts as Maslow's hierarchy of needs and values, and the concept of self-actualization, highlight the way in which people are understood to be responsible for their own success, so that those who do not achieve are equally considered to be responsible for their own failure. This failure can result in the self-blame, low self-esteem and sense of inadequacy that are the most common themes in work with women clients. These models are based on the white middle-class, and as with so many models we have described, can be impervious to class, gender and race issues.

Conclusions

Feminist theorists are seeking to correct a tradition in psychological theory that goes right back to Aristotle's statement 'the female is a female by virtue of a certain lack of qualities: we should regard the female nature as afflicted with natural defectiveness'. These theorists seek to address the failure of previous theories of 'human development' to appreciate the relational nature of women's sense of themselves (Jordan 1990: 137). However, they have had to incorporate their ideas into a structure and framework already in existence. Dutton-Douglas (1988) and Walker (2001) draw attention to the fact that a comprehensive theory of women's development to inform and direct therapeutic practice is still lacking, although steps have been taken in that direction. As we write, a comprehensive theory has yet to be presented.

Nicola Barden tosses both traditional analytic theory and feminist revisions of it into the air, suggesting that we review our whole way of thinking about gender identity development. She says it has always been obstructed by preformed expectations and suggests that the wrong questions have been asked in the first place. The usual questions about how gender identity develops and is maintained conspire to avoid a deeper and more basic question: Is the only way to regard gender through *two opposing poles*? The developmental models accepted by all psychological theorists restrict both men and women by forcing them to identify themselves on one or other side of the sexual divide. This divide is 'in essence restrictive and does not permit a variety of expressions in either gender' (2001: 2). It seems inconceivable that we could review human personality development without that polarization of the sexes, which is deeply engrained in our psychological thinking. However, as Barden says,

perhaps this would 'open up the possibility of a multiform distribution of gender-based potentials whereby women and men are given
the freedom to express their gendered selves in an infinite variety of
ways' (2001: 2).

Cultural factors in personality development

Val Simanowitz

In this chapter we have deliberately concentrated upon black identity and the implications of various studies in this field for thinking
about personal development. As we are (or have been) trainers on
Counselling Diplomas in inner-city contexts, where usually at least
half the students are black, we have thought it essential to be aware
of the black perspective throughout the training and to integrate
specific transcultural modules, as well as transcultural awareness,
throughout the course. In terms of the development of personality
we are aware that not only does the black person have the usual
tasks of psychological development within his or her own family,
and the norms therein, but also within a society which, in the case
of Europe and North America, is one that is dominated by white
and Western values, and where the issue of *visibility* is constantly
present. These values, often influenced by overt, subtle or internalized
racism, have informed research into and writing about developmental strengths and weaknesses, and notions of maturity and
psychological health.

> At a drop-in youth project in Eastbourne, a town with a predomin-
> antly white and elderly population, two black young women came
> (separately) for counselling and saw two white volunteer counsellors
> for more than a year. Tzala (aged 19) had been sent alone from
> Zambia to a boarding school in Eastbourne when she was only 14.
> After this move any home life was non-existent. She was severely
> bulimic, but told nobody about it and felt very lonely and isolated.
> Azuma (aged 21) was born in London of Nigerian parents who
> already had a large family. She had been separated from her siblings

at the age of 11 and sent to Eastbourne to a white foster home without any explanation. She suffered from low self-esteem, felt unloved and lonely. Both girls were successful academically and had done well on courses in higher education in tourism and computer skills. Both girls were depressed and had little sense of themselves, but did not identify the fact that they were black as any part of the problem. And neither did the volunteer counsellors. Later, Azuma's counsellor Sally began to work with her on this issue. According to the model of racial identity development described below, both girls had remained in the early (pre-encounter) stages of racial identity development, either unaware or in denial of the significance of race in their lives.

Culture is accorded great significance in both Erikson's stage theory and the reformulation of Piaget's developmental progression theory. However, its significance for the development of a distinctively black identity and the consequent implications for transcultural counsellors only developed with the raising of black awareness in the United States in the 1960s and 1970s.

Jackson, in *A Handbook of Multicultural Counselling* (Pontoretto *et al.* 2001), charts the absence of a specific awareness of black cultural identity in the early counselling and guidance movements and in theoretical approaches. In line with theories of white superiority in the 1940s and 1950s, an awareness of black identity was not included in contemporary counselling developmental theories and practice. Indeed, often the principal goal of white counsellors with black clients was to integrate them into the mainstream culture. Before 1960 there were few articles on minority culture in counselling journals and a number of black people found that the articles they did submit to such journals were not published. Between 1952 and 1959 only five articles that addressed the concerns of a multi-cultural clientele were published in *The Journal of Counselling*, but these laid the groundwork for the theories of racial and minority identity development that proliferated in the 1970s and 1980s.

Therapists began to realize that adaptive personal identity acquired in a specific cultural context is significant in terms of human choices and decisions. Therapists must recognize the importance of cultural learning as a crucial aspect of identity formation (Pederson *et al.* 1996). In addition, the theories of cultural identity that developed had to explain the phenomenon of moving up and down the developmental scale, rather than sequentially as in many other developmental theories.

In the United States there have been many theories (some of which have been revised and updated) charting the development of black and ethnic minority awareness. They describe the psychology of becoming black, or what was often called Nigrescence. Some of the earlier theories (Cross 1971; Thomas 1971) focus on the development of black identity in adults, but later writers such as Phinney (1989, 1993) and Atkinson *et al.* (1989) extend the discourse to include adolescent identity development.

The Cross model (1971) is one of the best-known and well-reviewed models of Nigrescence, but by 1995 Baldwin and Taylor had researched its limitations (Cross 1995). They decided that the self-hatred dynamics, which were perceived as part of the pre-encounter stage, are not as strong as had been envisaged and that some people probably have an identity that gives low salience to race as compared with other influences. They also decided that the 1971 model, which stressed self-healing and ideological unity as a result of Nigrescence, was not necessarily true. They thought that advanced black identity might be as much associated with Black Nationalism as with biculturalism or multiculturalism. In the light of these findings Cross decided to revise his model. Here we describe that revised model (which includes many of the salient aspects of other black identity models) and its relevance for white counsellors working transculturally. ('The Psychology of Nigrescence – Revising the Cross Model' from *A Handbook of Multi-cultural Counselling*, Pontoretto *et al.* 2001: 93.)

The revised Cross model of the development of black identity

The model basically describes how black people transform a non-Afrocentric identity into an Afrocentric one, in five stages.

Stage 1: the pre-encounter stage

Cross starts by observing that this stage transcends class boundaries and may be identified in a range of social classes from the black middle-class professional to the inner-city dweller.

At this stage black people's attitude to race encompasses low salience or race neutrality as well as being anti-black. People do not deny their physical blackness but consider blackness plays an insignificant role in their lives. Some of them have given the matter little thought, or have prioritized other influences, such as the Church, in their lives.

Azuma, removed from an inner-city black family environment at the age of 11 and placed with a white foster mother in an all-white English seaside town, tried to conceal her blackness. She felt she was ugly and tried to hide herself and her face behind a curtain of hair. When she first came for counselling she occasionally managed to peep out from behind the fringe, but she could not make eye contact with the counsellor.

In the pre-encounter stage, some see race as a stigma, and the only meaning of their racial identity is linked to the suffering of discrimination. Some people, dominated by negative racist stereotypes, believe these are true and loathe other blacks. They also believe that blacks deserve their misery and their poverty, as it arises from being intellectually inferior and technologically backward. Many black people are educated to embrace the Western cultural and historical perspective and are not aware of the significance of black experience. They are brought up with a Eurocentric cultural perspective and equate only Western culture, such as ballet and European art, with 'high' culture.

Some black artists in the pre-encounter stage are anti-black, perceiving white art as that which is positive, rational and highly developed and black art as primitive, exotic and emotional. Thus classical music, ballet and Western theatre define 'good' art, whereas jazz, blues and African dance are seen as primitive and inferior.

Some blacks in the pre-encounter stage have an anxiety about their 'race-image' even though many have not internalized some of the prevailing stereotypes. Though they themselves have not accepted the stereotypes, they are very aware that most white people have and are hypersensitive and constantly on the lookout for negative remarks or images. This sensitivity can also lead to a concern about things being 'too black'. Cross calls this 'spotlight anxiety'. It can lead to a desire for blacks always to be on their best behaviour and not act loud or disorderly. If whites are around, the person is hyperaware of the impression other blacks are giving and whether they are failing to project the best race image.

Azuma liked some of the bright fashions that her contemporaries in London wore, but she always dressed in sober muted colours when she was in Eastbourne for fear of being noticed.

Cross describes anti-black blacks as 'enslaved in a body and community they hate. They have a sense of imposition, alienation and inferiority' (Cross 1995). Through miseducation and a faith in the established system, blacks often see themselves as victims who are also to blame and that the solution to their conflict lies in assimilation and integration into the prevailing white culture. They think the onus is on them to become accepted by whites. Once they have adapted to fit in, then whites can be asked to stop discrimination, but they accept that it is the black people themselves who need to adapt and change.

Although Cross's earlier model stated that pre-encounter black people have different value structures from black people in the more advanced stages, he now believes that the value structure between those in the pre-encounter stage and those in advanced stages of identity development may not be so different. People in the pre-encounter stages often have strong commitments to religious and other secular organizations and are extremely altruistic. However, the commitment of pre-encounter blacks is likely to be to organizations where race has a low priority, whereas blacks in advanced stages of identity development will be involved with organizations in which black issues and culture are important. For example, on one London counselling course, black students were often committed members of black evangelical churches, but they did not want to discuss race as an issue in counselling training, claiming it was not important and they were on the course to learn theory and skills.

Cross stresses that pre-encounter black people, even the self-hating ones, are not mentally ill. They are separated from other Afrocentric blacks by value-orientation, historical perspective and their worldview (which is not usually formed by a pro-black or Afrocentric perspective). He maintains that pre-encounter black people must be understood as part of the diversity of black experience. They are also ripe for a possible identity conversion.

Stage 2: the encounter stage

As stability and predictability are important factors in preserving identity, it is often only the advent of some particularly traumatic or unexpected event that can bring about change. The encounter must 'work around, slip through, or shatter the relevance of the person's current identity and worldview' (Cross 1995). In many cases it is not a single event but a series of small events that begin to infiltrate a person's awareness and push them towards Nigrescence. Although most black people are exposed to a series of racist events in their lives, it is only when they experience such events as relevant to them, or personalize one of them, that the event becomes significant. For example, a diminutive and gentle black male student described how he was running for a bus one day when he noticed that two old ladies in front of him started running too, emitting small shrieks. He realized that they thought he was a black mugger chasing them. This was a significant event in moving him into the encounter stage.

The significant event might be when the black person learns previously unknown powerful historical/cultural information about the black experience, which may challenge them to rethink their world-view.

After the encounter, first reactions may be painful, confused or depressing, there may be guilt or anger at the white world, and this often leads to a frantic search for black identity.

Stage 3: the immersion and 'emersion' stage

One predictable response to this new awareness is that people immerse themselves in the black world, energized by rage, guilt or pride. They will devour black culture, literature, film, music and art and any knowledge that is relevant to the black experience. For example, a young nurse who previously adulated Florence Nightingale replaced her pin-ups with pictures of the little-known black nurse Mary Seacole. The Afrocentric movement has led to an explosion in creativity so that people feel driven to write, compose and perform around black themes. Many black artists previously influenced by the Eurocentric culture think their new awareness of their blackness has opened them up 'to a vast new world of rich colours, powerful dramas, irony, rage, oppression and impossible dreams' (Cross 1995).

At the immersion stage communication with others, whether black or white, is often blunt, direct and confrontational. At its extreme it can lead to a constant judging and labelling of others and a competition with other black people in an 'I am blacker than thou' vein. Taken to an extreme this can have disastrous results and can lead to coercive fascist tactics, as in the well-documented split between Malcolm X and the Nation of Islam.

The new converts are highly anxious that their blackness is 'pure and acceptable' (Cross 1995: 106) and can be very conformist. Within black organizations people need to prove their blackness, and they often need to be seen to confront authority such as the police, sometimes on a life-or-death basis. If this impulse is linked to revolutionary ideology, organizations such as the Black Panthers evolve. During this stage black people often experience a surge of altruism and become completely dedicated to the ideal of black togetherness. The experience is often so strong it has a 'religious or spiritual quality' (Cross 1995).

'Emersion'

At this stage the person finds it hard to sustain the fervour and passion of the immersion stage. It begins to 'level off' and they feel more in control of their emotions and experience. The levelling off is often a combination of the person's own growth and an awareness of the behaviour of black role models. People realize that their first impressions are often romanticized and that this is a period of transition rather than an end state. This stage can have negative consequences as some people stagnate in it, particularly if their expectations fail, and sometimes the new spirit is broken. Some drop out in despair, considering the racist problem insurmountable. Some become depressed or break down. Some, however, feel stable enough to move on to the final stage.

Stage 4: internalization

At this stage people still give a high priority to their blackness. However, this new internalized identity has three extra functions in their daily lives. It defends them from the ubiquitous racial insults that exist in society; it provides a sense of belonging and social roots; and it provides a strong base for communication with people, cultures and situations that are not related to blackness. Internalization is not necessarily lifelong and may need to be recycled at various points in a person's life. However, the successful resolution of racial identity conflicts can free people to deal with other significant concerns in their lives, such as gender, religion, class and poverty.

Internalization can transform dissonance into harmony. Such people feel calmer, more relaxed and more at ease with themselves. They become less concerned with how others see them and develop an inner confidence. They move from rage with everyone and everything white to controlled anger towards oppressive systems. They move from an anxious, insecure 'pseudo-blackness based on hatred of whites' to positive black pride and self-love, and a sense of commitment to the connection with the black community. They move away from the simplistic to a deeper understanding of the complex nature of the black condition, and this can be a departure point for future analysis.

Such people perceive themselves as totally changed, with a new world-view and philosophy. The basis of the core personality, which has been under stress in previous stages, is established on a firm footing. Basic personality attributes are likely to remain the same, but the changes caused by belonging to a black social reference group are the most important elements affecting the person's life.

Although internalization leads to a high emphasis on race and culture, the degree still varies according to the person's character and the importance they afford to ideology. Some may become vulgar nationalists; some may subject their thinking to more rational analyses and debate; some will turn to a bicultural reference group and see their blackness in the paradoxical context of their nationality. They can separate out the positive aspects of the society they live in from the more negative ones, which they will reject.

Bailey Jackson (1976: 42) sees internalization as the balance of blackness with other aspects of one's personality, such as sexual identity, occupational or religious identities.

Cross's model was very much based on his own journey from 'Negro' student at Denver University in 1960 to Black community leader and academic. (It was also based on hundreds of interviews he conducted with black people in his first job in an all-white insurance company in Chicago.) In his early life (pre-encounter) he was not particularly aware of race and culture (he was very light skinned). He describes his meeting with the only other Negro student, Badi, his newfound awareness of the significance of their skin colour and the delight they found in realizing that they had both come from the same district in Chicago. 'Two Negro strangers face to face as if each had discovered a pot of gold.' Badi was to become his lifelong friend and mentor and the person who invited him to teach at Princeton University, inspiring him to write his 1971 model of black identity. As a psychology student, Cross states that his model was subconsciously influenced by the process perspective that informs the stages of therapy, as well as by a religious deconversion during which he tried to unlearn his previously devout religious upbringing (immersion to emersion).

Some experiences that influenced the evolution and writing of his model were encountered in his job as the first black employee in an all-white insurance company. His role was to interview a range of black people, including community leaders, in order to develop an after-school project for black people that might help lessen the tension caused by recent race riots. He found each interview was like an intense seminar in black culture, and by the end of a year he felt he had completed a masters degree in black studies. The death of Martin Luther King was his trigger (his encounter) and his resultant rage made it impossible for him to function in an all-white world. Inevitably, his anger at work caused him to be sacked, and he became a community leader, a director of a centre set up to diffuse black anger, in Chicago. 'On a personal level I was rolling out to Encounter and dropping head first – body twisting arms flailing both fists clenched, Afro growing an inch a day – into Immersion-Emersion' (Cross 2001: 34). His spare time was spent increasing his knowledge about black American culture in lectures and seminars run by the Organization of Black American Culture (OBAC). As a result his black identity model became one that combined elements of 'how one can live and negotiate imposed notions of race' and 'how one can learn to embrace blackness as ethnicity or culture' (2001: 35). At that stage he also learned a great deal from a group of unofficial black panthers (whom he perceived as men of the street destined for prison) who shared his building.

He saw himself as a failure as a community leader, but then was invited by Badi to teach on an African-American Studies programme at Princeton University. Here he encountered black people who had reached the internalized stage of identity development. In response to negative images of black militancy in the media he was encouraged to express his view that black people were going through a process and to write and publish his model, which became a blueprint for many who followed and a subject of research.

By 1991, it seems he himself had reached the stage of internalization. He wrote *Shades of Black*, a sociological, historical and cultural treatise on black identity and psychological development. In it he attempted to focus away from black negativity, self-hatred and pathology onto a new nexus of identity variability and transformation. He wanted to show that (apart from the underclass) blacks have usually been able to achieve adequate levels of psychological functioning and identity development. He stressed that blacks do not have a single definition of what it means to be black nor what it means to live the good black life. In the light of these conclusions he revised some of the findings of his original model, which was more relevant for the 1970s than the 1990s.

Other models of black identity

Practitioners developed numerous models of black racial identity in the 1980s and 1990s, many along similar lines to Cross's. Atkinson *et al.* (1989) propose a five-stage model of minority identity development, which is very similar to Cross's model but is applicable to all ethnic minority groups.

Sabnani *et al.* (1991) formulate a model of majority identity development, which delineates the majority group's developing identity in relation to other minority groups. In the final stages, the white Anglo-Saxon majority members redefine themselves by acknowledging their own oppressive attitudes, thoughts and feelings; and become integrated enough to challenge other forms of oppression. This model is important for the development of therapist awareness: therapists who wish to work transculturally can aim towards the final stage.

In 1984 Janet Helms drew up a stage model of racial identity that she later updated (1990). She decided to replace the concept of stages, which she found inadequate for describing the developmental processes, being too strongly fixed and inflexible, with that of statuses of the ego. Her ego status models of people of colour racial identity (Table 9.2. 186. *Handbook of Multicultural Counselling*) and of white racial identity (Table 9.1. 185) bear a close resemblance to Cross, Atkinson *et al.*, and Sabnani.

It is clear that there is a Western cultural bias in both the theory and practice of therapy. Therapeutic and counselling training is informed by the cultural, class and ethnic background of the theorists and trainers. Western assumptions are accepted as given, resulting in various negative consequences such as racism, sexism, ageism and homophobia.

As Lago and Thompson point out in *Race, Culture and Counselling* (1996), counselling has generally been accepted in our society as a 'subtle but powerful ritual on the cutting edge of change'. They point out that the principles of all rituals develop in response to emerging trends but lose effectiveness over time. They consider that the current forms of counselling are still too greatly influenced by past theories of personality development and therapeutic practice, which are not an adequate response to the changes and contemporary needs of society.

Paul Pedersen's ten frequent assumptions of cultural bias in counselling

In 1987 Paul Pedersen outlined 'ten frequent assumptions of cultural bias in Counselling'. He considers that all counsellors should have awareness of how many of these assumptions they share and whether these are beneficial, harmful or irrelevant for the client sitting in front of them. These assumptions have relevance for attitudes to personality development, and they include the following:

- Counsellors, clients and researchers share a universal definition of the normal, where variations are perceived as deviations in order to protect the status quo.
- There is an emphasis on individualism, self-awareness and self-fulfilment and on the counsellor's task of helping the individual change, even if it is to the detriment of the group.
- Academic discipline, research and teaching are fragmented by artificial boundaries. Thus counsellors are encapsulated in their own 'discipline' and do not gain from other branches of knowledge, as well as being unaware of cultural variables. They assume that abstract words and concepts are universally understood.
- There is an overemphasis on independence and a lack of understanding of the significance of dependence in other cultures.
- There is a neglect of the client's own support system and a wish to replace it by paid professional help.
- There is a dependence on linear thinking, a cause-and-effect way of understanding the world. Tests, assessment interviews and measures are given considerable importance.
- Counsellors often change individuals to fit into the system rather than attempt to change the system. Counsellors should recognize when counselling could be more activist and change the system to fit the individual. They can be seen as agents of the system and could at least question whether the best interests of the clients are served by existing institutions and how far they can effect any change.
- Counsellors have a tendency to focus on the present and lack any knowledge of how people solved psychological problems in the past. Counsellors can be perceived to lack respect for tradition.
- Counsellors may promote dominance by the elitist groups unless they are prepared to challenge their own assumptions.

As counsellors and therapists who work transculturally in this multicultural society, we need to address the assumptions described by Pedersen, and a knowledge of the stages or statuses of racial identity development can assist this task. The following example demonstrates what lack of such knowledge can do to understanding a client.

> *A trainee counsellor was working with Nuala. Nuala was born of Indian parents in India and arrived in Britain aged 7. At age 23 she rejected her family's wish to arrange a marriage, and influenced by a Western education left home, rented a flat and kept herself by working part-time while trying to study in higher education. She had been in the pre-encounter stage in her late and early teens, but she now wanted more awareness of her Asian identity, although at the same time she rejected some of her family's traditional values. The trainee counsellor thought he was empathizing by encouraging her wish for independence and self-fulfilment and by supporting her strong criticisms of her family. He did not key into her grief and loss, or the significance of her Asian identity. It took three or four months before he was aware of being 'out of tune' when the client said she did not feel heard. He realized how Western assumptions were influencing his practice. Then he started to empathize with her conflict and her strong wishes to reclaim her family: it was only at that point that he was truly in relationship with his client and deeper work could begin.*

We have, in chapter six, also looked at issues about gender. Taken together these two chapters demonstrate the need for much more careful research and theorizing about what constitutes personality development, so that models of personality development not only take account of inbuilt factors such as gender, race and sexual orientation, but also study specific developmental tasks within particular sectors of society. We have concentrated in this chapter on black issues, with examples from African and Asian cultures; but it may well be that within the large group of 'white' clients, too, we need to take specific factors into account, particularly where national or religious values influence developmental models, implicitly or explicitly.

C H A P T E R **8**

Transpersonal and psycho-spiritual psychology

Jarlath Benson

Transpersonal and psycho-spiritual psychology includes and extends the view of personality development described in previous chapters.

The psychodynamic approaches associated with Freud and his followers look back to the earliest stages of life to understand how the basis of ego development and its later manifestations are laid down in the individual and this school has been neatly termed by the leading transpersonal theorist Ken Wilber as *prepersonal* psychology (1990: 215–60). The humanistic and person-centred approaches of Maslow, Rogers and others are more concerned to describe healthy ego functioning, growth, quality and responsibility and are summed up by Wilber as *personal* psychology. In *transpersonal* and *psycho-spiritual* psychology the individual ego is still present but is transcended and re-contextualized as the individual becomes increasingly preoccupied with ethical and spiritual concerns, realization of and expression of the essential self and with higher values, purpose and meaning, intuition, creativity and imagination.

It was William James who first used the term *transpersonal* in 1905. James, who was a leading figure in American intellectual thought and a founding father of modern psychology, sought to legitimize the study of the entire range of human experience, including religious experience, mystical states, psychic phenomena and non-Western conceptions of personality and consciousness. James's most significant contribution to the psychology of spirituality was his analysis of mystical consciousness, first published in *The Varieties of Religious Experience* (1902) in which he argued that the importance of mystical experiences was not least their capacity to increase the moral and aesthetic quality of life and enhance and transform interactions between people.

Carl Jung and the spiritual dimension

Carl Gustav Jung was an early and hugely significant colleague of Freud but split from Freud in 1913 on various theoretical grounds. Jung strongly disagreed with Freud that religion was a neurosis, a throwback to childhood fears that should be set aside as development to adult life proceeds. Jung regarded religion as psychologically necessary for mental wellbeing, particularly in the second half of life and for societal cohesion. He rejected the Freudian thesis that neurosis was a consequence of repressed sexual and aggressive conflicts and stated that: 'A psychoneurosis must be understood ultimately as the suffering of a soul which has not discovered its meaning.' (West 2000: 25)

By introducing here the idea of the soul and the importance of meaning as the critical factor in healing psychological distress, Jung recontextualized psychology as sacred psychology and promoted a religious attitude, relation to God and the cultivation of a spiritual life as essential for healthy personal growth and development.

Throughout his writings Jung repeatedly insists that he is not talking about God as absolute being since this is unknowable but rather is asserting the psychodynamic experience and image of the numinous or divine and how this has been expressed by people in various God-images.

Jung is a psychologist and not a theologian and emphasizes that human beings have a unique ability to formulate positive and negative God-images that represent the most potent values within the individual psyche. Jung believes that the essence of psychic nature is a disposition to God and a religious attitude that attests to the psychological necessity of religious experience, whether that is devotion to a traditional god, patriotism for country, fervour for one's football team, pursuit of success or any other form that orders people's lives and provides them with meaning and purpose.

Jung's views on the collective unconscious and the structure of personality are examined more closely in other volumes in the series (Edwards and Jacobs 2003, Brinich and Shelley 2002). But it is important to stress that the self represents the integration and perfection of the personality, which results from a continuing process of development that Jung calls *individuation*, or the inherent drive of the human being to become fully whole according to its nature.

Individuation as a developmental process involves differentiating and integrating such various components of personality as the *ego* (the organizing principle of the conscious mind), the *shadow* (the repressed unconscious aspect of the individual), the *persona* (the social mask adopted in response to demands of the environment), and the *animus* and *anima* (masculine and feminine opposites within the person). Together with mastery of the psychological functions of *thinking, feeling, sensation* and *intuition*, these gradually come under the conscious control of the self, which constitutes the newly re-centred ego so that the person attains self-realization and becomes an individual with a full sense of psychic wholeness.

The profound contribution of Jung's analytical psychology to the development of transpersonal psychology is that it makes primary the role of the spiritual in human affairs and brings soul and spirit properly back into the consulting room, thereby hugely and significantly expanding the range of enquiry and possibility for the counsellor-psychotherapist and the client-patient and providing invaluable concepts and techniques for psychological work.

Roberto Assagioli and psychosynthesis

Roberto Assagioli (1888–1974) developed psychosynthesis, which while sharing much with Jungian psychology differs in many import-ant points. It is Assagioli's view that the development of the indi-vidual was not only an end in itself but a means to an end. He believes that in the person there is a natural progression towards synthesis – a principle of sophisticated interdependence which means creating higher-level organizations and wholes both within the individual and between and beyond individuals.

Synthesis is a dynamic towards wholeness and emergence that reconciles the everyday experience of multiplicity with the familiar desire for unity. It is an intra-psychic and inter-personal and trans-personal organizing principle: '. . . the spirit working upon and within all creation . . . shaping it into order, harmony and beauty, uniting all beings . . . with each other through links of love, achieving slowly and silently but powerfully and irresistibly – *the Supreme Synthesis*.' (1975: 31, original italics)

Assagioli is clear that: 'Psychosynthesis definitely affirms the reality of spiritual experience, the existence of the higher values and of the "noetic" or "noological" dimension.' (1975: 195) The aim of psycho-synthesis is: '. . . to include within the study of psychological facts all those which may be related to the higher urges within man which tend to make him grow towards greater realizations of his spiritual essence.' (1975: 193)

He defines spiritual:

> We are using the word spiritual in its broader connotation which includes therefore not only the specific religious experience but all the states of awareness, all the functions and activities which have as common denominator the possessing of values higher than the average such as the ethical the aesthetic, the heroic, the humanitarian and the altruistic.
>
> (1975: 38)

Assagioli is certain that: '. . . the spiritual is as basic as the material part in man.' (1975: 193)

The principle of synthesis is seen clearly in the process and development of increasing *consciousness* and *will* in individual personality formation. Psychosynthesis asserts that the essential human identity is that of a spiritual self, and that this self exists as an ontological reality. It is pure being and the stable centre of life. Assagioli's assertion of the ontological reality of the self is quite different from Jung's view of the self as an archetype or primordial idea which appears to emphasize a more conceptual and abstract principle of psychic regulation.

What Assagioli means is that in the state of self-realization our experience of ourselves is a pure act of consciousness. We are not identified with the past or any mental construct or trying to be other than who we spontaneously and genuinely are at that moment. There is no effort to be oneself and no need to *do* anything to be ourselves. We are ourselves. We simply and completely are. The individual can and frequently does have direct experience of the self in unbidden altered states of consciousness such as joy, ecstasy, play and intuition, and there is also of course a psychological journey to be made to arrive at who we essentially are and have always been. Certain features of that psychological journey are well described by psychoanalytic ego psychology but assume quite a different emphasis in psychosynthetic developmental theory.

Assagioli's developmental views have been expanded by Joan Evans and Jarlath Benson at the Institute of Psychosynthesis, London, and are briefly summarized here. (Evans 1995; Benson 2001; Evans 2003)

In the first stage of development the ego is the initial expression of self in matter and successful ego formation is the primary task of infancy. The ego is a psychological vehicle or medium for the self and enables the self to physically incarnate in the world. The ego has a degree of consciousness and is a structure built out of life's experiences, fed by desires and instincts, complete with defence mechanisms, reacting to the environment and ensuring survival, but it is not yet conscious of the self that it is. Because of normal and pathological processes of identification with physical, emotional and mental aspects of its experience the ego can incorrectly take itself to be the source of our being not understanding that it is the means that we have to express who we essentially are. The ensuing psycho-spiritual journey of the person through the life cycle is the usual method of correcting this mistaken identity.

The second stage of synthesis is the awakening to self in matter or the emergence of 'I' consciousness and purposefulness. Usually around adolescence and onwards the personal self or sense of 'I' begins to constellate. This experience of 'I-ness' provides a sense of identity and continuity even though our everyday experience of ourselves and the world is constantly changing and evolving. Will and intentionality is a function of the emergence of 'I' identity and the evocation and activation of the will is a vital factor in its development. Since the will is a direct expression and capacity of individuals to function freely according to their own intrinsic nature rather than under the compulsion of external forces, a conscious act of will is one of the most powerful ways of experiencing oneself as a self-directing being, a free and responsible agent initiating and regulating action in contrast to submitting passively to it, and so much psychosynthetic therapy is oriented to evoking aspects, qualities and stages of will expression.

The experience and development of will is intimately linked with moral and ethical questions and the formation of a value system that guides behaviour, so it is no surprise that the 'I' increasingly aligns with the self that it essentially is. This third stage of development is referred to in psychosynthesis as the stage of *self-realization* – the gradual consciousness that one is centrally and essentially a self. This is usually a task of maturity and adulthood and results in the experience and belief that the individual's highest values extend beyond the purely personal: that they are aligned in action, service and compassion with the social and global spirit of the times and that the person's psychological journey is inextricably intertwined with the greater journey of mankind. Thus there is a psycho-spiritual context that not only serves to restructure and reorient personality but provides the basis for faith and belief that the purpose and goals that are emerging are indeed resonant with Spirit.

In summary, then, one can say that psychosynthesis involves the thorough knowledge and control of one's personality, the realization of one's true self and finally the re-formation or reconstruction of the personality around this new centre.

Ken Wilber's levels of consciousness and the pre/trans fallacy

Ken Wilber is perhaps the leading transpersonal theorist and has developed a model of human growth and development that integrates Western psychology and philosophy with Eastern concepts of personality and consciousness. His *spectrum of consciousness* model outlines a series of developmental stages in which various tasks and achievements must be sequentially completed before the person can progress to the next stage (1980). This linear model is based on a graduated ascent from the most primitive lower states of consciousness to higher mystical experiences, and finally to an ultimate state of being achieved by very few but theoretically available to all.

Wilber has distilled the 17 basic levels or structures that make up the realms of matter, body, mind, soul and spirit into seven stages and three realms (1998). The first stage he calls the 'archaic' stage and this includes the material body, sensations, perceptions and emotions. This is roughly equivalent to Jean Piaget's description of sensorimotor intelligence and Abraham Maslow's depiction of physiological needs. If the self develops poorly at this stage the individual may suffer psychotic disturbances in subsequent life, but if the self develops normally it progresses smoothly to the next stage. Wilber calls the second stage of growth the 'magical' world-view because the earliest mental productions and rudimentary concepts display condensation, displacement and 'omnipotence of thought'. This stage is similar to Freud's concept of primary process and Piaget's preoperational thinking and is correlated to Lawrence Kohlberg's stage of pre-conventional morality and Maslow's safety needs. Disturbance at this stage will lead to narcissistic and borderline pathologies. The third stage is called the 'mythic' and while more advanced than the magic stage the self is not yet capable of clear rationality, hypothesizing or deductive reasoning. It is similar to Piaget's concrete operational thinking, Kohlberg's conventional stages and Maslow's belonging needs. Difficulties here can lead to psychoneurosis. The fourth stage of development is called the 'rational' because the evolving self can not only think but also think about thinking. It is thus introspective and capable of hypothetical reasoning and testing. This stage is equivalent to Piaget's formal operational thinking, Kohlberg's post-conventional morality and Maslow's self-esteem needs. The fifth stage of human growth is called by Wilber the 'psychic', which does not necessarily mean paranormal but refers more to the beginning of transpersonal, spiritual or contemplative development, imagination, vision and the life of the soul. Maslow would describe this stage as concerned with self-actualization needs. The sixth stage is the 'subtle' or intermediate stage of spiritual development and is concerned with intuition and illumination. It correlates to Jung's archetypal level and the start of Maslow's self-transcendence needs. The seventh stage is called the 'causal' in that it is the limit of growth and development and is the 'ground of being' described by Tillich (1952).

Wilber has further condensed his evolutionary model of consciousness into three very useful ways of differentiating reality – the prepersonal, the personal and the transpersonal. As we have seen, each of these levels has its own developmental achievements and failures, and different schools of psychotherapy and philosophical systems have evolved to deal with the demands of the particular realm of reality. This insight does away with competition between the schools and systems of thought and demonstrates convincingly that various schools have particular expertise and competence within their own domain.

Wilber has also contributed a powerful analysis of common confusions between prepersonal and transpersonal experience and phenomena which he calls the pre/trans fallacy (1995). This is a very helpful concept for the clinician who is struggling to determine whether a particular individual is suffering from psychotic delusions or is genuinely experiencing spiritual insight. This fallacy or misinterpretation of phenomena has two major forms. In the first form transpersonal experiences are reduced to the operation of prepersonal psychological dynamics. Wilber sees Freud for all his undoubted merits as incorrectly and consistently collapsing genuine religious and spiritual experience into expressions of id, sex, emotion and nature, thus destroying the possibility of ego transcendence and higher-level wholeness.

Wilber asserts that the second form of the pre/trans confusion occurs when prepersonal phenomena are wrongly elevated to the status of transpersonal states of consciousness. Because Jung basically posits two major realms of personal and collective experience, Wilber believes that Jung frequently makes the mistake of fusing the two distinct dimensions, often 'glorifying certain infantile mythic forms of thought' and giving a 'regressive treatment of spirit'. It is significant that Wilber singles out Assagioli as not making pre/trans fallacies and this is because Assagioli introduces the intermediate agency of 'I' consciousness which can discriminate between prepersonal and transpersonal phenomena.

There can be little doubt that Wilber is a theoretician and model builder of the first rank and his ability to differentiate and integrate concepts has contributed hugely to the development of transpersonal and psycho-spiritual psychology and its increasing acceptance as the new paradigm in psychology. However, there has been trenchant criticism from John Heron, amongst others, that Wilber's model of the transpersonal and psycho-spiritual realm lacks dynamic polarity in that it emphasizes 'ascent' rather than 'descent' and is too uncreatively linear and hierarchical (Heron 2000).

Michael Washburn has compared the models of Wilber and Jung (Assagioli), concluding that they are two different paradigms that guide transpersonal theory and may reflect different cultural perspectives (1994). Washburn asserts that the Jungian (Assagiolian) paradigm views human development as following a *spiral* course of departure from and higher return to the origins of being. From this perspective the ego initially emerges from the deepest sources of the psyche and then separates itself from these sources during the first half of life which is the period of ego development and dominance. In the second period of life the ego returns to the deep regions of the psyche to be integrated with the ground of being on a more developed trans-egoic level.

By contrast, Wilber's model is, according to Washburn, rooted in traditional cognitive-developmental psychology and sees human development as proceeding in a straight line of ascent from pre-egoic levels to egoic levels to ultimate trans-egoic levels. Washburn calls this a *ladder* paradigm because it determines the path of development as a step by step ascent of a hierarchy of psychic structures such as cognition, moral consciousness and self structures which are only activated sequentially and then assert themselves as the new governing structures of the psyche. Washburn suggests that the spiral paradigm owes much to Jung's knowledge of Western spirituality and esotericism, while the ladder paradigm reflects Wilber's deep interest in Eastern spirituality, particularly Buddhism and Vedanta which emphasize linear progression in consciousness. Washburn's delineation of the contrasting paradigms of sacred psychology is a most useful guide and enables the counsellor/psychotherapist to locate different models of human development appropriately and select valuable insights in service of the client's particular trajectory.

James Fowler's faith development model

Another stages model that can be located within the ladder paradigm of human spiritual consciousness is the theory of faith development put forward by James Fowler (1981). This purports to represent how individuals develop cognitively, morally and spiritually in dealing with questions of transcendental reality and meaning. Fowler draws on the work of Piaget, Erikson (see Chapter two) and Kohlberg (see chapter five) to present a linear seven-step progression of faith from an 'undifferentiated' preverbal faith of infants to a 'universalizing faith' of mature adulthood. He sees faith as directed towards a person's object of highest value but is concerned to outline the process of faith rather than examine the content of specific belief systems.

These stages are:

1. **Undifferentiated faith:** infancy in which preverbal issues of love and trust, attachment and abandonment predominate.
2. **Intuitive-projective faith:** influenced by parental example and norms. Imagination predominates at this stage and the child can project its internal object world as devils or angels, punitive or benign God.
3. **Mythic-literal faith:** individuals absorb the stories, beliefs and practices of their group and understand them literally.
4. **Synthetic-conventional faith:** beliefs and values are deeply felt but unexamined and faith is conforming and obedient to authority.
5. **Individuative-reflective faith:** self-examination and critical reflection on beliefs and values leads to a more personalized and self-responsible faith system.
6. **Conjunctive faith:** re-integration of previously repressed aspects of self leads to rituals, beliefs and observances that energize the individual, who is increasingly able to include more diversity and tolerance.
7. **Universalizing faith:** synthetic perspective in which the person takes the universal point of view and identifies with humanity, transcendent moral and spiritual actuality, service and compassion.

This theory provides the clinician with a typical map of spiritual development, which may be helpful where a client is struggling with issues of faith and belief or is suffering from the effects of wounding by religious systems or hierarchies. It demonstrates that spiritual belief and growth is a process, which involves critically and responsibly evaluating one's faith and transforming religious meaning rather than clinging to sterile and fixed practices and rituals. This does not mean abandoning the authentic core of one's religious roots but expanding beyond the inhibitions and restraints associated with previous stages of one's personal experience and capacity for belief. Faith is seen as a dynamic process, which can enhance one's life and open up creative relational possibilities between people instead of distorting into a dividing and polarizing force.

Despite this Fowler has received criticism, most notably from Ford-Grabowsky, who argues that masculine and cultural biases result in Fowler focusing more on the cognitive dimension of belief as opposed to the emotional and affective dimensions and that the model concentrates more on the positive aspects of development and has little to say about the role of deception, guilt and sin as obstacles to the development of faith (1987).

Jacobs (1993) criticizes the model from a different position: that it is too tied to stages; that it artificially creates a seventh stage when six will do; and that it does not represent sufficient fluidity in the way that people think and believe differently even within the same belief system. In his latest book on the subject he proposes five modes of belief which tie in well with progressive psychoanalytic thinking (2000).

Psychological crisis and spiritual emergence

Much of the work of the spiritually attuned psychotherapist revolves around the relationship between psychological crisis and spiritual awakening. The basic point is that much psychological crisis is the egoic experience of the soul's need for expansion and expression – in other words, much personal distress is an indication of a basic need to redefine one's identity. Lacking a spiritual context or vocabulary, many people find their problems and dissatisfaction with their lives is only exacerbated unless they can encounter a perspective, which encourages them to re-align and orient their lives according to their deepest values. What brings many people to counselling or psychotherapy is a conscious need to relieve their distress and an unconscious need to expand their identity, discover their will and develop, whether in relation to others, themselves or to a higher Self – the precise terms depend upon the school that is defining the objective (see also Syme and Elton, forthcoming).

Assagioli believed that psychological crisis often preceded and indeed caused a spiritual awakening and that spiritual awakening could also provoke psychological disturbance by stirring up repressed and unresolved aspects and complexes in the personality. He was clear that the regressive and progressive features of such crises required careful discrimination if the spiritual emergence and the psychological disturbance were not to be mistaken for each other and incorrectly and unhelpfully mistreated.

Most psychological approaches aim at personality adjustment, managing psychopathology and correcting developmental failures: they omit a transpersonal dimension. For the transpersonal therapist such a limited view stifles the possibility of recontextualizing the psychological distress and reconfiguring one's sense of self around a new and expanded spiritual centre of identity. The transpersonal therapist believes that limiting the possibility of spiritual emergence caused by the therapist's inability to see and cooperate with what is really trying to emerge can induce a new trauma in the patient's life (Grof and Grof 1989).

Transpersonal and psycho-spiritual psychology has a distinct world-view and conception of the development of the human being. It asserts the primary importance of the spiritual dimension in human life and postulates that human consciousness is more and broader than any previous psychology has believed. It sees the root of much personality distortion and suffering as resulting from inadequate attention to this realm and views reductive explanations of human development and psychopathology as one-sided and unhelpful. Transpersonal psychotherapy involves working with and integrating body, mind, soul and spirit, thereby recognizing and honouring the 'biopsychosociospiritual' organism-continuum that is the human being and the human condition.

C H A P T E R **9**

Conclusion

Peter Pearce and Val Simanowitz

In this book we have covered a wide and somewhat bewildering array of models of the development of personality, and in the course of doing this have ourselves been impressed by the beauty, wisdom and symmetry of some of the theories. At the same time our attempt to re-engage with the concepts and to identify salient and significant aspects of the theories has given rise to numerous questions about the veracity of many of the elements we have considered. Further investigation has highlighted glaring omissions and has stimulated questions and doubts about the degree of efficacy of such theories as they influence our work with vulnerable and disturbed clients.

It seems that some therapist practitioners, particularly trainees or those who yearn for structure, have used personality theories in a quasi-religious manner, allowing them to guide their work with a blind faith in their rightness as if they are incontrovertible realities. This behaviour gives succour to the pronouncements of many a commentator that therapy has replaced religion as a means of guiding us on moral as well as psychological issues. Indeed, many of the leading developmental theorists themselves have at times been almost evangelical in their promulgation of their theories, brooking no divergence or opposition. Freud scornfully dismissed Karen Horney when she questioned his theories as being phallocentric, value-laden and representing the interests of men (Walker 2001: 55). He blamed her views on personal lack of awareness of the 'intensity of her own desire for a penis' (Kelman 1967: 26).

We also contend that by sticking rigidly to their theories of personality development, therapists may miss out on other perspectives, which could be equally illuminating. Spinelli provides an interesting example of this by describing a demonstration session given by Carl Rogers in South Africa (Spinelli 1994: 271–5).

> *Jan, a 35-year-old woman, expressed her fears of marriage and chil-dren and her fears of ageing. She wanted to devote herself to her love of music and dancing and feared that marriage and children would pre-vent this and she would end up a bitter and frustrated woman like her mother, who had died aged 53. She also feared being trapped. Rogers suggested that, while admired by her friends on the outside as some-one who had it all, inside she was a different person. Jan admitted to being the 'Naughty little girl'. She also expressed a lack of someone special to relate to in her life. Rogers suggested 'maybe one of your best friends is the you that you hide inside, the fearful little girl, the naughty little girl, the real you that doesn't come out very much in the open.'*

Here Rogers is keying in to his belief in a 'real organismic self'. Spinelli disagrees with Rogers' view that the naughty little girl is Jan's real self and feels that Rogers missed out by not giving equal weight to the adult, fearful Jan, whom Spinelli sees as an aspect of the 'unreal self'. In a fairly directive way (which seems to run contrary to the non-directive ethos implicit in person-centredness) he has chosen to pick up this theme rather than any other to work with. He introduces it spontaneously quite some time after Jan first mentions it.

However some of the theorists described in this book have made it clear that their theories are not set in tablets of stone. Levinson, for example, acknowledges that while his eras and developmental periods can be seen as discrete entities, there are overlaps and con-siderable interpenetration of one period by another; and that there are times throughout the life cycle which contain elements of other periods.

There are other limitations to personality theories. Many of them are hierarchical, reflecting a patriarchal, heterosexual and simplistic view of development rather than a fluid and flexible one that acknow-ledges diversity. Freud, for example, saw the satisfactory completion of one developmental stage as a pre-requisite for development to mature adulthood, where the person can achieve heterosexual fulfil-ment. This has been used by some of Freud's later followers (even until 1995) to decide that homosexuals should not be trained as ana-lysts or therapists, as they could not be available for the transference relationships in the heterosexual area (Murrain 2000: 110). This caused immense pain at the time.

Erikson's and Levinson's stage theories also broadly see development as progressive, and that the person needs to reconcile polarities and achieve tasks in order to advance to a higher stage. In his six-stage theory Kohlberg describes what a person needs to do to reach a mature and high level of moral development. The person is expected to progress from level 1, conforming to the rules to level 6, where the person can differentiate themselves from the rules and define values in terms of principles they have considered and adopted for themself. Spiritual/faith models too, for example that by Fowler, conceptualize the development of faith and the development of the spiritual in terms of stages and levels, which progress from the lowest to the highest. In Fowler's model, growth is cumulative. A person must complete each discrete stage before moving on to a higher one. These models pose questions around those who do not take a linear path, who do not progress or who may even regress from a higher to a lower level during their spiritual journey.

We find that the idea of developmental life stages can be mirrored in views of how the therapist develops. During Rowan's and Jacobs' debate on the therapist's use of self (in this series, 2002) they focus on the development of the authentic. While Rowan condenses his earlier thinking into a theory of three levels: 'the instrumental, where the emphasis is all on getting it right; the authentic, where the emphasis is on being real: and the transpersonal, where the emphasis is on surrender to something larger' (Rowan and Jacobs 2002: 116), Jacobs does not like the idea of levels.

> I am unhappy . . . about thinking of these as levels: as though we ought to progress from one to the other in our development as therapists. I can see a clear place for all three ways of being, probably in every session, as adaptations to where we were with a particular client at a particular time.
>
> (Rowan and Jacobs 2002: 117)

While the structure of all stage theories has a marked similarity in terms of being linear and hierarchical, the concepts used to describe personality development are also found across a range of approaches. For example, Fairbairn's description of external relationships being taken in to become part of ourselves as 'internal objects' (Fairbairn 1954) has parallels with the Rogerian development of the 'self-concept' and Kohut's building of 'self-structure' (Kohut 1971). Similarly the 'actualizing tendency' (Rogers 1963), the 'inherited potential' or 'true self' (Winnicott 1958) and the tendency to 'enhance and order functioning through the experience of the self' (Kohut 1971) seem closely related concepts. There appear to be parallels too in the process of the infant being met with 'maternal attunement' (Winnicott 1958), which gradually reduces through manageable 'failures' in the caregiver's adaptation, and Kohut's (1971) suggestion that healthy development occurs when both 'gratification' and 'frustration' are optimal. These are just a few of the many concepts that have some measure of compatibility. However, although the terms may have similar meanings, the focus of different theories is often fundamentally different. For example, in general terms, psychoanalytical approaches highlight the essentialist and determinist elements of personality, particularly the negative, destructive and aggressive instincts and drives, while humanists focus more on the positive aspects of our personalities and the human thrust towards growth and change.

Another limitation of theories of personality development is that many of them omit or only pay lip service to the later stages of life. Freud, Klein and other analytical therapists focused almost exclusively on infancy and childhood. Indeed, Freud saw little point in looking at later stages of life because he thought it was difficult or impossible for people past the age of 40 to change or grow. While Erikson developed an eight-stage theory covering the life span he still focuses more on early stages, particularly adolescence. Levinson's 'stages of a man's life' seeks to address this by focusing his in-depth study of 40 men aged between 30 and 45, but he still neglects the periods of later middle age and old age.

Theories of personality development have justifiably been criticized for neglecting or ignoring the significance of the historical, social, cultural and political context that gave rise to them. The focus is so intra-personal that writers often seem unaware of how much they are influenced by the class, age, race and gender attitudes of their own backgrounds. Erikson attempted to address this by placing his subjects in relation to society but as his model is psychodynamic he was still influenced by Freud's patriarchal attitudes and focused on autonomy and separation as the pinnacles of success. Levinson, despite apologies, based his ten-year research project solely on men. It is not surprising, therefore, that the theories (like many aspects of therapy) may have a lack of relevance for oppressed groups such as those who live on run down housing estates in Southwark or Bradford, or migrant workers in the US who are struggling with the daily exigencies of earning their bread in a very unequal society.

Carl Rogers, warning against theoretical dogma, predicts that in the fullness of time all the theories we hold so dear will be superseded by new theories.

> If theory could be seen for what it is – a fallible, changing attempt to construct a network of gossamer threads which will contain the solid facts – then a theory would serve as it should, as a stimulus to further creative thinking.
>
> (Rogers in Koch (ed.) 1959: 191)

As Barden suggests, perhaps the very basis of some accepted theories, such as seeing gender as a form of opposing polarities, needs to be questioned and re-examined (2001: 13).

The current trend towards evidence-based approaches in mental health, and motivators like cost-effectiveness, have tended to focus both practitioner and research attentions alike on relationship and process issues in therapy sessions and away from less tangible developmental models. Many of the theories described here demand a degree of faith as in concrete terms they are unproven.

Despite such healthy scepticism, however, we are aware as authors that in practice, our theoretical orientations can sometimes be enhanced by relevant insights from developmental theory. As a person-centred therapist Val's work with a client was not only guided by Rogers' ideas about conditions of worth but was illuminated by Erikson's eight-stage life cycle theory:

Teresa was in her early 50s. She had, as a single parent, brought up two sons (who were both at university), had overcome alcoholism, and had succeeded in gaining an Open University degree. However, she was now beset by problems of depression, severe isolation, and very low self-esteem, by an inability to make relationships and by lack of employment or meaning in her life. She had been emotionally and physically abused throughout her childhood and adolescence and her parents had never valued or supported her. She had spent some time in mental hospitals and had been sexually abused by a therapist who had become her lover and had then abandoned her. Obviously she had almost intractable problems with trust. For months she found it difficult to trust the therapist. She pushed the boundaries, trying to phone between visits and attempting to come more often while declaring her strong feelings for her therapist. Eventually, once the therapist had resisted all her attempts to diverge from a professional relationship, while at the same time attempting to remain empathic, accepting and consistent, Teresa began to trust her. The

therapist was helped by Erikson's views that sometimes it is import-
ant to go back to early stages. Together they re-explored Teresa's early
years (stage 1: trust versus mistrust) and tried to work at the recon-
ciliation of opposing forces. They worked through some of the trauma
of her childhood, enabling her to exonerate herself from blame.
Teresa tentatively began to risk trusting new people she encountered in
her life. After 18 months of therapy she was able to organize the sale
of her house and a move to a new area to be near a friend. Of course,
many of her problems remained but she felt less depressed and more
positive about her future. She had gained some insights about the
source of her difficulties and felt more in charge of getting on with
her life.

Similarly Kohut's developmental ideas enriched Peter's work with
Ann, a 20-year-old woman with a learning disability, who was
taking a course in gardening at her local college. Ann sought help
through her doctor as she was having frequent episodes of panic,
anxious depression, hopelessness and suicidal thoughts. She lived at
home with her father, who was a recovering alcoholic, and with her
mother, who was herself on medication for depression having experi-
enced several earlier breakdowns. In therapy it was quickly apparent
that Ann had very harsh internal introjects. She was very demanding
of herself and anticipated that her counsellor would be equally hard
on her. She expected the counsellor, like her parents, only to value her
conditionally for her achievements. The counsellor consistently
attempted to meet Ann with the person-centred 'core conditions'
(Rogers 1958) and modelled her development in person-centred terms.
Her 'self-concept' seemed very fragile. Any sense of self-worth that she
did have seemed to depend largely upon her fulfilling others' expect-
ations of her, particularly those of her own needy parents. She had a
very externalized 'locus of evaluation' (Rogers 1951) and carried
around her own, internalized versions of this conditional valuing.
These harsh and oppressive 'conditions of worth' (Rogers 1959) made
her very demanding of, and judging about, herself. In Kohut's terms
Ann's developmental needs seemed to centre around the 'traumatic
frustrations' (Kohut 1971) of unshared emotionality, particularly in
her awareness of being different and disabled. Holding this awareness
helped the counsellor to be more closely attuned to when he might be
responsive to some of Ann's self-object needs and to recognize her
great need for such responses, so that she might increase her ability to
find self-objects of her own. For example, amid all her anxieties, the
counsellor was impressed by the depth of her understanding about

gardening and her obvious enthusiasm for this work. He fed this back to Ann. She came to sessions straight from college with her course books and picked up enthusiastically on this role of the knowledge-able one, taking the counsellor through her textbook and clearly finding such mirroring affect attunement (Kohut 1978) extremely affirming. Over time her preoccupation with eliciting confirmation from others that she was acceptable began to decrease. She gradually gained some confidence in her own abilities to cope and in what Kohut (1978) described as her capacity to self-soothe. She became markedly less reactive and more able to hold onto her own sense of worth in response to perceived criticism. She also began to share things that were going well.

Despite the many reservations we still have about aspects of the models we have described, personality development theories can help to illuminate how we come to be the way we are, and can aid insight into our clients as they proceed on their inner journeys. Indeed, many of the ideas put forward by Freud and those who followed him, whether of his school or any other, are already embedded in our thinking processes both consciously and unconsciously. Once upon a time these models might have been described as maps, although as we look at them now they are more like the rough representations of the early explorers rather than the precise charts of the cartographer. Today the image might not be so appropriate, because the develop-ment of human personality takes place on more than a two-dimensional plane. There are few fixed points, and people's journeys are, for them as individuals, often into the unknown. The models provide some reassurance to the guides (such as therapists) that others have charted the terrain, but the inner world of personal history is like a shifting landscape, and caution is necessary about reliance on those who have gone before. But if we use these models in a wise and discriminatory way, aware of all their limitations, they can still be a useful framework in the joint endeavour to overcome the distress, disturbance, confusion and difficulties that have usually brought clients to therapy.

We remember ourselves, looking back on the theories mapped out in previous chapters, that with some exceptions (notably Levinson, Kohlberg, Gilligan and Fowler) research into personal development from a psychotherapeutic perspective comes mainly from working with clients. While it is no doubt influenced by cultural norms (which is where the research in the general population may be more representative), it has of course often been with a specific population – those who have defined themselves or have been defined by others as in some way distressed or disturbed psychologically. Cultural norms have not always exercised an influence – we think of Freud's theory of psychosexual development as being the antithesis of what people generally believed of children, and of his criticism of civilized society and sexual morality. But it has nearly always been the case that in the first instance the client or patient has provided the yardstick. Thus theories of personality development have arisen by generalizing from the particular – always a danger. Nevertheless there is one lesson from this that is worth emphasizing. It is that ultimately it is by listening to the client, no doubt on many levels, that therapists learn about the development of the particular individual, learning which sometimes (but not always) may assist in relation to working with other clients. As authors from a person-centred perspective, it is encouraging to be able to commend in conclusion listening to the individual history of the client first and foremost, and only through that to construct what may be a working model of personality development, capable of adaptation to each and every one of those who choose to share their story.

References

Abraham, K. (1924) A short study of the development of the libido, viewed in the light of mental disorders, in *The Selected Papers of Karl Abraham* (1979) pp. 408–501. London: Karnac.

Ainsworth, M. (1982) Attachment: retrospect and prospect, in C.M. Parkes and J. Stevenson-Hinde (eds), *The Place of Attachment in Human Behaviour*. London: Tavistock.

Assagioli, R. (1975) *Psychosynthesis: A Collection of Basic Writings*. Wellingborough, Northants Turnstone Press.

Atkinson D. R., Morten G., and Sue D., (1989) *A minority identity development model 'Counselling American Minorities'* Dubuque, IA: William C. Brown.

Barden, N. (2001) The development of gender identity in S. Izzard. and N. Barden (eds), *Rethinking Gender and Therapy. The Changing Identities of Women*. Bucks: OU Press.

Barden, N. and Izzard, S. (eds) (2001) *Rethinking Gender and Therapy. The Changing Identities of Women*. Buckingham: OU Press.

Barrett-Lennard, G.T. (1998) *Carl Rogers Helping System: Journey and Substance*. London: Sage.

Benjamin, B. (1988) *The Bonds of Love: Psychoanalysis, Feminism and the Problem of Domination*. New York: Random House.

Benson, J.F. (2001) Chap.12. Working more synthetically with the group, in *Working More Creatively with Groups*. London and New York, Routledge.

Berne, E. (1961) *Transactional Analysis in Psychotherapy*. New York: Grove Press.

Binswanger, L. (1958) in May, R., Angel, E., and Ellenberger, H.F. (eds) *Existence: A New Dimension in Psychiatry and Psychology*. New York: Basic Books.

Binswanger, L. (1963) *Being-in-the-World Selected Papers of Ludwig Binswanger*. New York: Basic Books.

Blos, P. (1967) 'The second individuation process of adolescence', in A. Freud (ed.) *The Psychoanalytic Study of the Child Vol. 22*. New York International Universities Press.

Bowlby, J. (1969) (1981) *Attachment and Loss. Vol. 1. Attachment*. Penguin Books.

Bowlby, J. (1998) *A Secure Base. Clinical applications of attachment theory*. Tavistock/Routledge.

Brinich, P. and Shelley, C. (2002) *The Self and Personality Structure*. Open University Press.

Broverman, I., Vogel S., Broverman D., Clarkson F., and Rosenkrantz P., (1972) 'Sex-role Stereotypes: A Current Appraisal', in *Journal of Social Issues* 2, 859–78.

Cashdan, S. (1988) *Object Relations Therapy. Using the relationship*. New York: Norton.

Chaplin, J. (1998) The rhythm model, in Heenan, C.M. and Seu, B.I. *Feminism and Psychotherapy*. London: Sage.

Chasseguet-Smirgel, J. (1970) *Female Sexuality: New Psychoanalytic Views*. Ann Arbor: University of Michigan Press.

Chodorow, N. (1974) *Femininities, Masculinities, and Sexualities: Freud and Beyond*. London Free Association Books.

Chodorow, N. (1978) *The Reproduction of Mothering*. Berkeley, CA: University of California Press.

Chodorow, N. (1989) *Feminism and Psychoanalytic Theory*. Cambridge: Polity.

Cooley, C.H. (1902) *Human Nature and Social Order*. New York: Scribner's.

Cooper, M. (2000) 'Developing the Person-Centred Theory of Development' in *Person-Centred Practice* Volume 11, 87–94.

Cross, W.E. Jr. (1971) The Negro to Black Conversion Experience. *Black World*, pp. 13–27.

Cross, W.E. Jr. (1995) The negro-black conversion experience. *Black World*, 20, 13–26.

Cross, W.E. Jr., Parham, T., and Helms, J. (1995) Nigrescence revisited: theory and research, in R. Jones (ed.) *Advances in Black Psychology*, 1–69. Hampton, VA: Cobb and Henry.

De Beauvoir, S. (1952) *The Second Sex* Trans J.M. Parshley. New York: Vintage 1974.

Dewey, J. (1954) *Moral Principles of Education*. New York: Philosophical Library.

Dinnerstein, D. (1976) *The Rocking of the Cradle and the Ruling of the World*. USA: Harper and Row.

Durkheim, E. (1961) *Moral Education*. Glencoe, Ill.: The Free Press

Dutton-Douglas, M. (1988) *Feminist Psychotherapy: Integration of Therapeutic Systems* New Jersey: Ablex publ.corp

Eichenbaum, L. and Orbach, S. (1983) *Understanding Women: A Feminist Psychoanalytical Approach*. New York: Basic Books.

Erikson, E.H. (1956) The problem of ego identity, in *Journal of the American Psychoanalytic Association* 4, 56–121.

Erikson, E.H. (1965) *Childhood and Society*. London: Penguin.

Erikson, E.H. (1968) *Identity: Youth and Crisis*. New York: Norton.

Erikson, E.H. (1985) *The Life Cycle Completed*. New York: Norton.

Erikson, E.H., Erikson, J.M., and Kivnick, H.Q. (1989) *Vital Involvement in Old Age*. New York: Norton.

Evans, J. (1995) Psycho-spiritual psychology in *Self and Society*.

Evans, J. (2003) The triphasic model in Vol. 4 *Psychosynthesis Therapeutic Counselling*. Anamcara Press.

Fairbairn, W.R.D. (1952) *Psychoanalytic Studies of the Personality*. London: Routledge

Fairbairn, W.R.D. (1954) *An Object Relations Theory of the Personality*. New York: Basic books.

Fairbairn, W.R.D. (1963) Synopsis of an object relations theory of the personality, in *International Journal of Psychoanalysis*. 44: (224–225).

Ford-Grabowsky (1987) Flaws in Faith Development Theory, in *Religious Education*. Vol. 82 (181–83).

Fowler, J. (1981) *Stages of Faith: The Psychology of Human Development and The Quest for Meaning*. New York: O.U.P.

Frankl, V. (1955)(1973) *The Doctor and the Soul. From Psychotherapy to Logotherapy*. Pelican Books.

Frankl, V. (1959)(1985) *Man's Search for Meaning*. Washington Square Press.

Freud, A. (1963) The concept of developmental lines, *Psychoanalytic Study of the Child*, 18: 245–265.

Freud, A. (1998) *Anna Freud Selected Writings*, edited by Ekins, R. and Freeman, R. Penguin Books.

Freud, S. (1905) (1962) *Three Essays on the Theory of Sexuality*. London: Hogarth Press.

Freud, S. (1920) Beyond the pleasure principle, in *The Complete Psychological Works of Sigmund Freud*. SE18, pp. 1–64 London: Hogarth Press.

Freud, S. (1923) (1991) The infantile genital organisation, in *Penguin Freud Library*, Vol. 7.

Freud, S. (1924) (1991) The dissolution of the Oedipus complex, in *Penguin Freud Library*, Vol. 7.

Freud, S. (1925a) Some psychological consequences of the anatomical distinction between the sexes, in *Freud: Sexuality and the Psychology of Love* ed. P. Rieff 183–193. New York: Collier, 1963.

Freud, S. (1925b) (1991) Some psychical consequences of the anatomical distinction between the sexes, in *Penguin Freud Library*, Vol. 7.

Freud, S. (1933) New introductory lectures on psychoanalysis, in *The Complete Psychological Works of Sigmund Freud*. SE22, pp. 5–157. London: Hogarth Press.

Freud, S. (1938) (7th impression) *New Introductory Lectures on Psychoanalysis*. Hogarth Press.

Freud, S. (1940) (1971) An outline of psychoanalysis, from *The Complete Psychological Works of Sigmund Freud*. SE22, pp. 37–39. London: Hogarth Press.

Gay, P. (1988) *Freud: A Life For Our Time*, New York: Norton.

Gilligan, C. (1982) *In a Different Voice*. Cambridge Mass: Harvard University Press.

Golan, N. (1981) *Passing Through Transitions*. New York: Free Press.

Grof, S. and Grof, C. (1989) *Spiritual Emergency*. New York: Penguin.

Guntrip, H. (1971) *Psychoanalytic Theory, Therapy, and the Self*. New York: Basic Books.

Hazler, R.J. and Barwick, N. (2001) *The Therapeutic Environment*. Open University Press.

Heenan, C.M. and Seu, B.I. (eds) (1998) *Feminism and Psychotherapy*. London: Sage.

Helms, J.E. (1990) *Black and White Racial Identity: Theory, Research and Practice*. Westport, CT: Greenwood.

Heron, J. (1998) *The Sacred Science: Person-centred enquiry into the Spiritual and the Subtle*. Ross-on-Wye: PCCS.

Holmes, J. (1993) (2002) *John Bowlby and Attachment Theory*. Brunner Routledge.

Horner, M.S. (1968) Sex differences in achievement motivation and performance in competitive and non-competitive situations. Ph. D Diss. University of Michigan.

Horney, K. (1922) On the genesis of the castration complex in women, in *Feminine Psychology* (ed.) Kelman, 37–53. New York: Norton, 1967.

Jacobs, M. (1992) *Sigmund Freud*. London: Sage.

Jacobs, M. (1995) *D.W. Winnicott*. London: Sage.

Jahoda, M. (1950) Towards a social psychology of mental health, in Symposium on the Healthy Personality, Supplement II: Problems of Infancy and Childhood, Transactions of Fourth Conference, March 1950, M.J.E. Senn (ed.). New York: Josiah Macy, Jr. Foundation.

James, W. (1902) *Varieties of Religious Experience*. New York: Longman.

Jordan, J.U. (1990) Relational development through empathy: therapeutic applications, in *Empathy Revisited: Work in Progress*, no. 40, pp. 6–10. Wellesley, Ma: Wellesley College, Stone Centre.

Jung, C. (1958) *Psychology and Religion*. London: Routledge

Kahn, M. (1991) *Between Therapist and Client. The New Relationship*. New York: W.H. Freeman and Co.

Kant, I. (1952) The critique of pure reason, in *Great Books of the Western World*, 42. Chicago Encyclopedia Britannica.

Kaplan, A.G. (1990) Empathy and its vicissitudes, in *Empathy Revisited: Work in progress*, no. 40, pp. 6–10. Wellesley, Ma: Wellesley College, Stone Centre.

Keller, E.F. (1985) *Reflections on Gender and Science*. New Haven: Yale University Press.

Kelman, H. (1967) *Feminine Psychology*. New York: Norton.

Kobasa, S.C. and Maddi, S.R. (1977) Existential personality theory, in R.J. Corsini (ed.), *Current Personality Theories*. Peacock Publishers: Itasca, Ill.

Koch, S. (ed.) (1959) (1989) *A Psychology: A Study of Science*, Vol. 3, *Formulation of the Person and the Social Context*, New York: McGraw Hill, pp. 184–256.

Kohlberg, L. (1976) Moral stages and moralization: the cognitive–developmental approach in T. Lickona, (ed.) *Moral Development and Behaviour: Theory, Research and Social Issues*. New York: Holt, Rinehart and Winston.

Kohlberg, L. (1981) *The Philosophy of Moral Development*. San Francisco: Harper and Row.

Kohlberg, L. and Kramer, R. (1973) Continuities and discontinuities in childhood and adult moral development revisited, in *Collected Papers on*

Moral Development and Moral Education. Moral Education Research Foundation.

Kohut, H. (1971) *The Analysis of the Self*. New York: International University Press.

Kohut, H. (1978) (Ornstein, P. ed.) *The Search for the Self: Selected Writings of Heinz Kohut, 1950–1978*. New York International University Press.

Kohut, H. and Wolf, E.S. (1978) The disorders of the self and their treatment: an outline. *International Journal of Psychoanalysis*, 59: 413–26.

Kovel, J. (1988) *The Radical Spirit*. London: FA Books.

Lago, C. and Thompson, J. (1996) *Race, Culture and Counselling*. Bucks: Open University.

Lever, J. (1976) Sex Differences in the Games Children Play, in *Social Problems* 23: 478–89.

Levinson, D.J. (1978) *The Seasons of a Man's Life*. New York: Basic Books.

Loevinger, J. (1976) *Ego Development: Conceptions and Theories*. Jossey Bass.

Maddi, S.R. and Kobasa, S.C. (1984) *The Hardy Executive: Health Under Stress*. Dow-Jones-Irwin: Homewood, Ill.

Maddi, S.R. (1996) *Personality Theories. A comparative analysis*. 6th edition. Brooks/Cole.

Mahler, M.S. (1968) *On Human Symbiosis or the Vicissitudes of Individuation*. New York: Basic Books.

Mahler, M.S., Pine, F., and Bergman, A. (1975) *The Psychological Birth of the Human Infant*. New York: Basic Books.

Marrone, M. (1998) *Attachment and Interaction*. London: Jessica Kingsley Publishers Ltd.

Maslow, A.H. (1954) *Motivation and Personality*. New York: Harper and Row.

Maslow, A.H. (1964) Religions, Values and Peak Experiences. New York: Penguin Books.

May, R. (1953) *Man's Search for Himself*. New York: Norton.

May, R., Angel, E., and Ellenberger, H.F. (eds) *Existence: A New Dimension in Psychiatry and Psychology*. New York: Basic Books.

May, R. (1967) *Psychology and The Human Dilemma*. Princeton, N.J.: Van Nostrand.

May, R. (1969) *Love and Will*. New York: Dell.

May, R. (1981) *Freedom and Destiny*. New York: Norton.

May, R. (1983) *The Discovery of Being: writing in existential psychology*. New York: Norton.

Mearns, D. and Thorne, B. (1988) *Person-Centred Counselling in Action*. London: Sage.

Mearns, D. and Thorne, B. (2000) *Person-Centred Therapy Today. New Frontiers in Theory and Practice*. London: Sage.

Merry, T. (1999) *Learning and Being in Person-Centred Counselling*. Ross-on-Wye PCCS Books.

Miller, J.B. (1976) *Towards a New Psychology of Women*. Boston: Beacon Press.

Millett, K. (1969) *Sexual Politics*. Doubleday: New York

Mills, J. (1958) Changes in moral attitudes following temptation, in *Journal of personality* 26 (517–531).

Mitchell, J. (1986) *The Selected Melanie Klein*. Penguin Books.

O'Connor and Ryan (1993) *Wild Desires and Mistaken Identities*. London: Virago.

Oetting, E.R. and Beauvais, F. (1990) Orthogonal cultural identification theory: the cultural identification of minority adolescents, in *International Journal of Adiictions*, 25 (655–85).

Pedersen, P. (1987) Ten frequent assumptions of cultural bias in Counselling, in *Journal of Multicultural Development* Jan 1987.

Pedersen, P., Draguns, B., Juris G., Lonner Walter J., and Trimble Joseph, E. (1996) *Counselling Across Cultures*. London: Sage.

Phinney, J. (1989) Stages of ethnic identity development in minority group adolescents, in *Journal of Early Adolescence*, 9, 34–49.

Phinney, J. (1992) The multigroup ethnic identity measure, in *Journal of Adolescent Research*, 7, 156–176.

Phinney, J. (1993) A 3 stage model of Ethnic Identity Development, in M.E. Bernal and G. Knight (eds) *Ethnic identity: formation and transmission among Hispanics and Other Minorities* (61–79). Albany State University of New York Press.

Piaget, J. (1932) *Moral Judgement of the Child*. Free Press.

Piaget, J. (1976) *The Child and Reality. Problems of Genetic Psychology*. Penguin.

Piaget, J. and Inhelder, B. (1963) *The Child's Conception of Space Humanities*.

Pollak, S. and Gilligan, C. (1982) Images of violence in thematic apperception test stories, in *Journal of Personality and Social Psychology*. 42, 1: 159–167.

Pontoretto, J.G. and Casa, J.M. (1991) *Handbook of Racial and Ethnic Minority Counselling Research*. Springfield, Ill.

Pontoretto, J.G., Casas, J.M., Suzuki L.A., and Alexander, A.A. (2001) *A Handbook of Multi-cultural Counselling*. London: Sage

Prozan, C.K. (1992) *Feminist Psychoanalytic Psychotherapy*. Northvale: Jason Aronson Inc.

Rest, J., Turiel E., and Kohlberg L. (1969) Relations between levels of moral and preference and comprehension of the moral judgement of others, in *Journal of Personality* 37 (225–52).

Rogers, C. (1951) *Client-Centred Therapy*. London: Constable.

Rogers, C. (1959) (1989) A theory of therapy, personality and interpersonal relationships, as developed in the client-centred framework, in S. Koch (ed.) *Psychology: a Study of Science*, Vol. 111. *Formulations of the Person and the Social Context*. New York: McGraw-Hill. pp. 184–256.

Rowan, J. and Jacobs, M. (2002) *The Therapist's Use of Self*. Bucks: Open University.

Rycroft, C. (1968) (1972) *A Critical Dictionary of Psychoanalysis*. Penguin Books Ltd.

Sabnani, H.B., Pontoretto J.G., and Borodowsky, L.G. (1991) *White racial identity development and cross-cultural counselor training: a stage model*, in The Counselling Psychologist 19 (76–102).

Sartre, P. (1943/1956) *Being and Nothingness*. (trans. H. Barnes) London: Routledge.

Sassen, G. (1980) Success anxiety in women: A constructivist interpretation of its sources and significance. *Harvard Educational Review* 50: 13–25.

Segal, H. (1973) (1986) *Introduction to the Work of Melanie Klein*. Hogarth Press.

Sperry, L. (2001) *Spirituality in Clinical Practice: Incorporating the Spiritual Dimension in Counselling And Psychotherapy*. Brunner-Routledge.

Spinelli, E. (1994) *Demystifying Therapy*. London: Constable.

Spock, B. (1945) *The Common Sense Book of Baby and Childcare*: New York: Duell, Sloane and Pearce.

Stern, D.N. (1985) (1998) *The Interpersonal World of the Infant. A view from psychoanalysis and developmental psychology*. London: Karnac Books.

Stevens, R. (1983a) *Freud and Psychoanalysis*. An Exposition and Appraisal. Open University Press.

Stevens, R. (1983b) *Erik Erikson*. Milton Keynes: Open University Press.

Surrey, J. (1990) Empathy: evolving theoretical perspectives, in *Empathy Revisited: Work in Progress*, no. 40, pp. 6–10. Wellesley, Ma: Wellesley College, Stone Centre.

Symington, N. (1986) *The Analytic Experience. Lectures from the Tavistock*. Free Association Books Ltd.

Taylor, E. (1996) William James and transpersonal psychiatry, in *Textbook of Transpersonal Psychiatry and Psychology* (eds) Scotton, B.W., Chinen, A.B., and Battista, J.R. Basic Books. HarperCollins.

Thomas, C. (1971) *Boys no more*. Beverly Hills, CA: Glencoe.

Thorne, B. (1992) *Carl Rogers*. London: Sage.

Tillich, P. (1952) *The Courage to Be*. New Haven: Yale University Press.

Tong, R. (1989) *Feminist Thought: A Comprehensive Introduction*. London: Routledge.

Vaillant, G. (1977) *Adaptation to Life*. Boston: Little, Brown.

Walker, M. (2001) Adolescence: possibilities and limitations, experience and expression in S. Izzard. and N. Barden, (eds) *Rethinking Gender and Therapy. The Changing Identities of Women*. Bucks: Open University Press.

Warner, Margaret (1999) 'The language of psychology as it affects women and other traditionally disempowered groups' in Fairhurst, I. (ed.) *Women Writing in the Person-centred Approach*, p. 193. PCCS.

Washburn, M. (1994) Transpersonal psychology in *Psychoanalytic Perspective* pp. 12–13. State University of New York Press.

Welchman, K. (2000) *Erik Erikson, his Life, Work and Significance*. Buckingham and Philadelphia: Open University Press.

West, W. (2000) *Psychotherapy & Spirituality: Crossing the Line Between Therapy and Religion*. London: Sage.

Wilber, K. (1980) *The Atman Project: A Transpersonal View of Human Development*. Wheaton, Ill.: The Theosophical Publishing House.

Wilber, K. (1983) *Up From Eden: A Transpersonal View of Human Development*. London and New York: Routledge & Kegan Paul.

Wilber, K. (1990) The pre/trans fallacy pp. 215–60 in *Eye To Eye: The Quest for the New Paradigm*. Boston & Shaftesbury: Shambala.

Wilber, K. (1995) *Sex, Ecology, Spirituality: The Spirit of Evolution*. London: Shambala.

Wilber, K. (1998) The spectrum of consciousness, in *The Essential Ken Wilber: An Introductory Reader*. London: Shambala.

Winnicott, D.W. (1953) Transitional objects and transitional phenomena, in *International Journal of Psychoanalysis* XXXIV.

Winnicott, D.W. (1954) (1992) The depressive position in normal emotional development, in *Through Paediatrics to Psychoanalysis*. London: Karnac Books.

Winnicott, D.W. (1956) (1992) Primary maternal preoccupation, in *Through Paediatrics to Psychoanalysis*. London: Karnac Books.

Winnicott, D.W. (1960a) (1990) The theory of the parent-infant relationship, in *Maturational Processes and the Facilitating Environment*. London: Karnac Books.

Winnicott, D.W. (1960b) (1990) Ego distortions in terms of true and false self, in *Maturational Processes and the Facilitating Environment*. London: Karnac Books.

Winnicott, D.W. (1965) (1989) *The Family and Individual Development*. London: Tavistock/Routledge.

Winnicott, D.W. (1971) (1974) *Playing and Reality*. Harmondsworth: Pelican

Winnicott, D.W. (1987) *Babies and Their Mothers*. London. Free Association Books.

Winnicott, D.W. (1990) *The Maturational Processes and the Facilitating Environment. Studies in the Theory of Emotional Development*. London: Karnac Books.

Wolheim, R. (1971) *Freud*. Fontana.

Yalom, I.D. (1980) *Existential Psychotherapy*. New York: Basic Books.

Index

CONSCIOUS AND UNCONSCIOUS

David Edwards and Michael Jacobs

All forms of psychotherapy deal with the limitations of our awareness. We have limited knowledge of our creative potential, of the details of our own behaviour, of what motivates us, or of the many factors within and around us that influence the decisions we make and the ways we act. Some therapists, especially those influenced by Freud and Jung, speak of the 'unconscious', giving the unintended impression that it is a kind of realm or domain of activity. Others, reacting against the specifics of Freudian theory, shun the word 'unconscious' altogether. However, so limited is the reach of everyday awareness and such is the range of unconscious factors, that one way or another these limitations must somehow be spoken about, sometimes in metaphor, sometimes more explicitly. This book offers a broad survey of psychotherapy discourses, including the psychoanalytical, the interpersonal, the experiential, the cognitive-behavioural and the transpersonal, and explores a wide range of concepts including repressed instincts, dissociated selves, automaticity, tacit knowledge, unformulated experience, preontological concealment and interactive fields.

Conscious and unconscious is invaluable reading for advanced students of counselling and psychotherapy and experienced therapists.

Contents
Introduction – Constructing and deconstructing the unconscious – Conscious and unconscious in historical perspective – Freud, Jung and Alder – The development of alternative discourses: Harry Stack Sullivan, Fritz Perls and Medard Boss – Evolving psychoanalytic discourses of the unconscious – Conscious and unconscious in cognitive therapy and science – Invisible worlds, unconscious fields and the nonegoic core: evolving discourses of the transpersonal unconscious – Conscious and unconscious: integrative models and perspectives.

128pp   0 335 20949 1 (Paperback)   0 335 20950 5 (Hardback)

THE THERAPIST'S USE OF SELF

John Rowan and Michael Jacobs

. . . a masterful exposition of transference, countertransference, and projective identification, throwing much needed light on topics that have long been mired in controversy and confusion. The book is a priceless resource for experienced therapists and those just beginning the journey.

> Professor Sheldon Cashadan, author of Object Relations Therapy and The Witch Must Die: The Hidden Meaning of Fairy Tales

Rowan and Jacobs, each a master in his own field, have done a wonderful collaborative job. The book's focus on what different ways of being a therapist really mean in practice guarantees its relevance for therapists of all schools (or none) and at every level.

> Andrew Samuels, Professor of Analytical Psychology, University of Essex and Visiting Professor of Psychoanalytic Studies, Goldmith's College, University of London

This book is part of the series *Core Concepts in Therapy*, which takes important concepts in psychotherapy and counselling (which we call collectively therapy), and asks how they are used in different orientations. For this purpose each volume is written by two authors from contrasting approaches. The present volume deals with what is perhaps the central question in therapy – who is the therapist? And how does that actually come across and manifest itself in the therapeutic relationship? A good deal of the thinking about this in psychoanalysis has come under the heading of countertransference. Much of the thinking in the humanistic approaches has come under such headings as empathy, genuineness, non-possessive warmth, presence, personhood. These two streams of thinking about the therapist's own self provide much material for the bulk of the book – but other aspects of the therapist also enter the picture, including the way a therapist is trained, and uses supervision, in order to make fuller use of her or his own reactions, responses and experience in working with any one client.

The book is aimed primarily at counsellors and psychotherapists, or trainees in these disciplines. It has been written in a way that is accessible to students at all levels, but it is also of particular value to existing practitioners with an interest in the problems of integration.

Contents
Series editor's preface – Introduction – The instrumental self – The authentic self – The transpersonal self – Training and supervision – Dialogue – Bibliography – Index.

176pp   0 335 20776 6 (Paperback)   0 335 20777 4 (Hardback)

THE SELF AND PERSONALITY STRUCTURE

Paul M. Brinich and Christopher Shelley

- What is the self and its relationship to personality theories?
- How do the central schools of psychotherapy conceptualize the self?

The *self* is a notoriously difficult and at times obscure concept that underpins and guides much psychotherapy theory and practice. The corollary concept of personality is fundamentally linked to the concept of the self and has provided theorists and researchers in psychology with a more coherent set of principles with which to explicate the personal and attributional aspects of the self. The authors come from two quite separate schools of depth psychology (psychoanalytic and Adlerian) and provide an overview of the self and how it is conceptualized across the psychotherapies within various theories of personality. In addition to outlining some of the philosophical and historical issues surrounding the notion of selfhood, the authors examine classical and developmental models of psychoanalytic thought that implicitly point to the idea of self. The authors also outline Kohut's psychoanalytic *self psychology* in addition to Adlerian and other post-Freudian, Jungian and post-Jungian, cognitive, humanistic, and existential contributions to the self and personality structure.

Contents

128pp   0 335 20563 1 (Paperback)   0 335 20564 X (Hardback)